A CENTURY
OF WAR

A CENTURY OF WAR

The history of worldwide conflict in the 20th Century

David Miller

CRESCENT BOOKS
NEW YORK

An Elephant Editions book

© 1997 by Elephant Editions Limited

All rights reserved under International and Pan-American
Copyright Conventions.

This 1997 edition is published by Crescent Books,
a division of Random House Value Publishing, Inc.,
201 East 50th Street, New York, NY 10022.

Crescent Books and colophon are trademarks of
Random House Value Publishing, Inc.

Random House
New York • Toronto • London • Sydney • Aukland
http://www.randomhouse.com/

A CIP catalog record for this book is available from
the Library of Congress

ISBN 0-517-18440-0

8 7 6 5 4 3 2 1

The Author
David Miller, a former serving officer in the British
armed forces, having seen service from Europe to the
Falklands, comes from a family of military men.
He is a respected defense historian and analyst who
has written almost 30 books on weapons and warfare.
He has contributed to many international
defense-related journals, and is Editor of
Jane's Major Warships.

Credits
Editor: Ray Bonds
Design direction: Robert Mathias, Publishing Workshop
Design : Helen Mathias
Photo research: Tony Moore
Typesetting and color reproduction: SX Composing DTP
Printed and bound in Spain by Book Print, S. L.

--- **Jacket and front matter photos:** ---

Jacket front:
LEFT: Men of US 173rd Airborne Brigade
return sniper fire north of Ai Lao River,
March 1970.

RIGHT: An Israeli tank commander is
lifted from his Centurion tank which has
been ambushed by Syrians on the Golan
heights during the 1973 war.

BOTTOM: US 23rd Infantry, 2nd Division,
fire a 37mm gun during an advance
against German positions in WWI.

Jacket back:
TOP: A B-17 on a sortie over Gizo Island,
Solomons, October 5 1942.

CENTER: An American M1
demonstrates its speed over desert terrain
in the Middle East.

BOTTOM: USS *Maryland* (BB-46)
bombards Tarawa, November 20 1943.

Front matter:
PAGE 1: US Army 7th Division smoke
out Japanese on Kwajalein Island,
February 2 1944.

PAGE 3: Coalition armor on the move in
the Gulf War, 1991.

PAGE 5, TOP TO BOTTOM:
Australian infantrymen move through the
ruins of Chatto Wood, Ypres Salient, 1917.

UN Disengagement Force on the Golan
Heights, June 28 1974.

Tanks of the UN peacekeeping force in
Sarajevo, Bosnia, 1990s.

Missile test-launch from USAF B-2 stealth
bomber.

CONTENTS

INTRODUCTION

ABOVE: German infantry in the ruins of Stalingrad in 1942. Their World War Two experiences remain firmly in the minds of the Russian people.

The 20th Century has been a period of uninterrupted conflict. There have been two global conflicts – the First World War 1914-18 and the Second World War 1939-45 – both on an unprecedented scale. There have also been hundreds of other conflicts, ranging in scale from the Vietnam and Gulf Wars, both of which involved well over a million people, to tiny affairs involving perhaps several thousand. Indeed, it is doubtful if there has been one day in the century when there has not been at least one conflict somewhere in the world, and frequently many more.

War is a legal state in which two or more countries 'declare war' on each other over a specific incident and thereafter fight until either one side wins or they negotiate a settlement. Classically, a war was started by the formal delivery of an ultimatum by an ambassador, stating a complaint, specifying a remedy, and setting a deadline, past which, if nothing had been heard, a state of war was considered to exist ('Your country has invaded X; we give you four days to disengage and withdraw back across the border, or a state of war will exist between us').

The Twentieth Century has, however, seen a gradual disappearance of such niceties, as was so chillingly demonstrated on December 7 1941 when the first that the USA knew of a

state of war with Japan was when Japanese aircraft swept in over Pearl Harbor, dropping bombs and torpedoes. The most recent example was in Kuwait, where Iraqi troops took the tiny emirate by surprise on August 2 1990.

Definitions

Various terms are used to describe the different types of conflict, of which the more commonly used (in descending order of violence) are:

General war. A global conflict involving superpowers, with the strong possibility of escalating to nuclear war.
Regional war. An open conflict confined to a geographical area. Thus, the 1982 Falklands (Malvinas) War was confined to an area around the islands and did not extend to the South American mainland.
Limited war. An open conflict which is deliberately limited to the use of conventional weapons.
Insurrection. An armed uprising in open opposition to the established government. The Mau Mau campaign in Kenya in 1953-55 is an example.
Insurgency. A prolonged armed uprising in opposition to the established government. This

term was widely used between 1950 and 1980 to describe campaigns such as those in Malaya (1948-1961) and the Philippines.

Communist Revolutionary Warfare (CRW). A term devised in the 1960s to describe insurgencies in which the aim was to establish a Communist government. The term was devised by the US Special Forces in the 1960s and assumed the use of Mao Tse-tung's strategic principles.

Revolution. A sudden and total change in the way a country is governed, almost always involving violence, and usually of relatively short duration. It is usually confined to the centres of political power (eg, national and provincial capital cities); it will almost always involve rioting and destruction, and may involve the limited use of armed force: for example, Chinese Revolution (1911); Russian Revolution (1917).

Civil war. An armed conflict between large groups within the same country: for example, the Spanish Civil War (1936-39).

Guerrilla war. A type of warfare involving numerous small bands of combatants, using tactics which include ambushes and small-scale attacks. In the past, guerrilla warfare was carried out in the countryside, with the guerrillas using mountains, forests or jungle as hiding places. Modern cities are so complex and dense that a new type of 'urban guerrilla' has also appeared.

Rebellion. Organised and armed resistance to the established government.

Terrorism. A tactic used by small groups or individuals, involving the use of terror methods (ie, murder, bombing, hijacking) to attain a political objective. Terrorism may be the sole method used in a campaign of violence (as, for example, by groups such as the Baader-Meinhoff gang and the Red Brigades) or may

LEFT: US Navy battleship, USS *California* (BB-44) lies blazing in Pearl Harbor on December 7 1941 - the 'day of infamy' when Japan launched its abortive war against the United States.

ABOVE: No campaign has been fought under such continuously appalling conditions as First World War's Western Front. These Canadian infantrymen are in one of the most infamous areas of all – the mud of Passchendaele.

BELOW: A cruise missile lifts off from the decks of USS *Missouri* en route for Iraq's capital, Baghdad, during the Second Gulf War.

be used as part of an insurgency.

Coup d'etat. A violent and illegal change of government, engineered by a small group who, by careful targeting, take over power rapidly, using a minimum of force, and without popular participation. There have been frequent military *coup d'etat* where military leaders, using their monopoly in weaponry and disciplined manpower, have 'dismissed' civilian governments without any violence being used at all. For example, the overthrow of Prime Minister Ali Bhutto by General Zia ul-Haq in Pakistan on July 5 1977.

Most of these terms are somewhat imprecise, while some are interchangeable; for example, **insurrection, insurgency, rebellion** and **Communist Revolutionary Warfare**. Also, there are subtle distinctions between some of the terms: the definition **civil war**, for example, implies that the social fabric of a country has

split vertically, as happened in the American Civil War in the 19th Century, while **insurgency** implies a horizontal split (peasants versus landowners, poor versus rich, etc). There is also an implication of time in some of the terms; **revolution**, for example, is a short-term affair and if prolonged would become either an insurgency or a civil war.

In addition, there is a further type of use of force, which can be defined as a '**Superpower operation**'. This covers situations where a global or regional superpower carries out a military operation within its acknowledged 'sphere of influence', in order to ensure its own security or to reclaim territory it considers its own. Examples include: Soviet operations in Hungary (1956) and Czechoslovakia (1968); US operations in Grenada (1983) and Panama (1989); the Chinese operation in Tibet (1949-50); and the Indian seizure of Goa (1961).

This does not imply that all such operations

LEFT: Another type of conflict as Czech protestors confront bewildered Russian tank crews in the streets of Prague in 1968.

share the same ethical basis; obviously, some are more moral than others. Nevertheless, these operations share the characteristics that they are carried out by a superpower, with limited aims, within clearly defined geographical limits, and with little fear that another external power will interfere.

There have been so many conflicts in the 20th Century that this book cannot attempt to cover them all. What it does do is to describe the major conflicts and to give selected examples of each type of minor con-

flict in an endeavour to cover what has been a very troubled period in human history. The book is divided into four sections and within each section the wars are dealt with sequentially:

Section 1. Major international conflicts.
Section 2. Regional conflicts and major civil wars.
Section 3. Other conflicts.
Section 4. Outlook for conflict in the 21st Century.

MAJOR INTERNATIONAL CONFLICTS

ABOVE: The commanders of the International Force sent to deal with the Boxer rebellion in China. Nations represented included Austria-Hungary, Britain, France, Italy, Japan, Russia, and the United States, the latter being the only officer without a moustache!

Boxer War 1900-1901

Throughout the 19th Century a number of major international powers nibbled away at Chinese territory, winning one concession after another and humiliating a proud people. This sense of frustration and impotence eventually gave rise to the Society of the Righteous Harmonious Fists (the 'Boxers') who targeted their attentions on Christian missionaries and their converts, with protests from Western diplomats simply raising the temperature. China was ruled by the Dowager Empress Tzu Hsi whose government surreptitiously aided the fanatics, while claiming to the Western ambassadors that it was trying to control them.

The Westerners most vulnerable to the violence were the diplomats in the capital, Peking, whose legations were grouped together. Appreciating the danger, a small force of some 485 sailors and marines from the international fleet gathering off Tientsin was sent to protect them. Mob violence increased around the legations and the assassination of the German ambassador was the prelude to a siege, which commenced on June 20 1900. The Western diplomats, their marine guards and the Chinese converts were eventually driven into two small

areas: the British Legation and the Roman Catholic Cathedral, where they held out, but incurred heavy losses.

Meanwhile, the international fleet had assembled a larger force of some 2,000 men, which set out for Peking on June 10, but was prevented from making much progress and withdrew in face of much superior force back to its ships on June 26. The international force issued an ultimatum to the Boxers positioned in the Taku forts to surrender, but this was rejected, so an assault force was sent ashore. It captured the forts which were then used as the assembly area for an international expeditionary force, which would then go to Peking. By early August the force numbered some 2,500 Americans, 3,000 British, 800 French, 4,800 Russians, a number of Japanese, with others bringing the total to some 18,700.

The city and fort at Tientsin were captured on July 23 and on August 4 this 'Second Relief Expedition' started its march to Peking. They pushed aside a force of some 10,000 Chinese at Yang T'sun, where the French contingent was left to guard the lines of communication. The remainder of the force arrived outside the walls of Peking on August 13, where the Russians, who were in the lead at the time, attempted an

LEFT: The US Artillery under First Lieutenant Charles Summeral bombarding the doors at the Ch'i Hua Gate, which guarded the entrance to the Imperial City.

immediate rush on the Tung Pien gate, but they were thrown back with considerable losses. The next day a more coordinated attack took the city and the troops pushed on to relieve the sieges at the British Legation and the Cathedral.

On August 15 the Western force attacked the Imperial City and one of the notable features of the attack occurred when First Lieutenant Charles Summeral of the US Artillery walked forward under heavy Chinese small arms fire in order to draw a chalk cross on the Ch'i Hua gate as an aiming mark for his gunners. The Chinese defence collapsed, although the Westerners did not actually occupy the Imperial City until late December.

By this time more contingents were arriving, with a large German force under Field Marshal Waldersee arriving on September 12, but, apart from an opportunity for sacking and looting the war was over.

The brief Boxer War was important for two reasons. The first was that it intensified the Chinese resentment of their treatment by Westerners, a legacy which endures to this day. The second was that it was the first major multi-national force of the modern era. Command was sometimes assumed by the senior officer present, while during the Second Relief Expedition there was no commander at all, with success being achieved by cooperation. Eventually the German, von Waldersee, became the nominal commander by virtue of his field marshal's rank, although by the time he arrived there was little real action left.

Russo-Japanese War 1904-1905

A clash between Russia, thrusting eastward to the Pacific, and Japan, claiming increasing swathes of the mainland, was inevitable. In the event, it was the Japanese who struck first, attacking the Russian fleet at anchor in Port Arthur on the night of February 8 1904, followed by a similar attack on ships in Inchon harbor on the 9th. Setting a pattern to be followed by others during the 20th Century, the Japanese then issued a formal declaration of war on February 10.

Imperial Russia was not only ill-prepared and poorly equipped for war, but also suffered from bad luck. One example was when the new Far East Fleet commander, Admiral Makarov, started a series of successful sorties on April 8, but his flagship hit a mine on the

BELOW: Wounded Chinese soldiers after a battle with the Japanese Army. The Chinese Army was defeated in its clashes with outside powers in the 19th Century and the first half of the 20th, leaving a bitter and enduring legacy.

13th and was lost with all hands, including the admiral. Ashore, matters went badly from the first and a series of Japanese successes led to the investment of Port Arthur, where some 40,000 Russian troops were ensconced in a strongly defended position.

On August 10 the Russian fleet attempted to leave the besieged Port Arthur on orders from the Czar, but were cornered by the Japanese fleet under the redoubtable Admiral Togo. During the course of a closely fought fleet engagement the Russian admiral, Vitgeft, was killed and his fleet then broke up in confusion, most returning to Port Arthur. This was followed four days later by an engagement between the Russian Vladivostok squadron (three cruisers) and a Japanese squadron (four cruisers), in which one Russian ship was sunk and the other two escaped, for no Japanese losses.

The Imperial Japanese Navy now had full command of the sea, but did not have matters all its own way at Port Arthur, where Russian resistance in defence was typically strong. Four assaults were mounted between August 7 and November 1, in which both sides fought with great determination and the Japanese incurred heavy losses. The Japanese then reverted to inching forward, capturing one outpost after another until the starving Russian garrison was forced to surrender on January 1 1905.

A second, mobile front had been opened in June 1904 in Central Manchuria, where a series of battles resulted in a steady Japanese advance towards Mukden. The Russian forces under General Kuropatkin fought with great stubbornness and the outcome of the campaign was frequently in the balance, but the Japanese advance continued and after being outgeneralled at the Battle of Mukden (February 21 – March 10 1905) Kuropatkin pulled back.

The Russian government had decided to

BELOW: The main squadron of Admiral Togo's fleet engaging the Russian squadron off Vladivostok on August 10 1904 when the Japanese prevented the Russian fleet from escaping. Battle ensigns are flying and the last ship in the line is firing a full broadside.

reinforce its depleted Far East Fleet by despatching the Baltic Fleet, which left on its long voyage on October 15 1904. After many adventures the fleet left its last stop in Indo-China on May 14 and it met the Japanese on May 27 in one of the great naval battles of the century: Tsushima. The Russians had eight battleships, eight cruisers and nine destroyers, while the Japanese had four battleships, eight cruisers, 21 destroyers and 60 torpedo boats.

The Russian ships, however, were old, and both ships and crews were exhausted after their long voyage, while the Japanese had

LEFT: A Japanese officer inspects his platoon during the Russo-Japanese War, where the Japanese infantry frequently outfought their Russian opponents.

more modern and better maintained ships, and their men were fresher, better trained and better disciplined. The main battle was of short duration, lasting from early afternoon to nightfall, with Japanese mopping up continuing through the night. In the end the only Russian survivors were three destroyers which sought refuge in Manila, and one cruiser and two destroyers which reached Vladivostok. These were the only survivors of the fleet that had left the Baltic seven months previously. It was a naval battle whose impact was to be felt for many years to come, and not

only by the two combatants.

Tsushima spelt the end of the war, with formal termination coming in a treaty signed at Portsmouth, New Hampshire, USA, on September 6 1905. Internationally, it was the first major military defeat inflicted on a European power by an Asian power and within Russia the resulting humiliation and discord led eventually to the 1917 Revolution. In Japan it encouraged a feeling of self-confidence and supremacy which led inexorably to the attack on Pearl Harbor and thence to utter defeat in August 1945.

BELOW: A well dug-in Russian artillery battery awaits a Japanese target. From Czarist times to the present, Russian artillery has enjoyed a high reputation for efficiency and sound gunnery tactics.

RIGHT: A British trench in France, with weary soldiers grabbing some sleep, while a comrade keeps watch armed with his 0.303 inch Short Magazine Lee-Enfield rifle. The revetments and bridge indicate a sense of permanence.

BELOW: American troops operating Renault tanks in the Argonne region in France in September 1918, less than two months before the war's end.

First World War 1914-1918

Background

With hindsight, the First World War seems to have been inevitable. The preceding decade was characterised by armament races between the great powers (on land between Germany and France, and at sea between Germany and Great Britain), the weakness of the Austro-Hungarian Empire, and Russia's Balkan policy, coupled, in virtually all European states, with jingoistic nationalism. There had also been a series of small wars: between Italy and Turkey in 1912, and two Balkan Wars, the first from October 1912 to May 1913 and the second from June to August 1913.

In such a high pressure situation it needed only a small spark to ignite the explosion, which came with the assassination of the Arch-Duke Francis Ferdinand of Austria-Hungary in Sarajevo. In all countries involved, the generals and admirals insisted that the order be given to start the massive mobilisation and deployment processes, while popular jingoism also pushed the statesmen into ever more entrenched positions. Austria-Hungary declared war on Serbia on July 28, while Germany declared war on Russia on August 1 and on France on August 3, which was accompanied by the invasion of Belgium. Great Britain joined on August 4 and Japan on August 24. Turkey declared itself an armed neutral, but when two former German warships flying the Turkish flag bombarded Black Sea ports, Russia, Britain and France declared war on Turkey between November 2 and 5.

Western Front

Germany was faced with a two-front war against France and Russia and started in accordance with the Schlieffen plan, remaining on the defensive in the east, while carrying out a broad right sweep through Belgium in the West. The German commander-in-chief, von Moltke, however, weakened the right wing, and the French were eventually able to halt the German advance and then start pushing them back. There then developed the 'rush for the sea' as the Anglo-French forces tried to get around the Germans' right flank but by November a single continuous front stretched from the Swiss frontier to the North Sea coast and the era of trench warfare had begun.

There then ensued three years of remorseless struggle in the West as the two sides sought a way out of the impasse. Technological innovations were introduced one after another: bigger guns; ever more efficient ways of controlling artillery; gas; huge mines; and tanks to name a few. Each provided a temporary advantage, but none provided the sought-for recipe for success. There were tactical innovations as well: solid lines; infiltration by 'storm troopers'; attacks preceded by massive artillery bombardment or by no preliminary artillery at all. The battles were on an unprecedented scale, involving more troops and lasting longer than any battles in history – and with much greater casualties. Names such as Ypres, Verdun, the Somme, became seared into the national consciousness of all the countries involved.

1915 and 1916 were devoted to periodic attempts by first one side then the other to break the deadlock, but these usually petered out with minor territorial gains, achieved only after massive losses. The epic struggle at Verdun lasted from February to November 1916, in which the French and Germans lost vast numbers of men. The true numbers will never be known, but are estimated to be approximately 435,000 German and 540,000 French, and all for very little gain; indeed, at the end it was the French that held the field. In an endeavour to ease the pressure on Verdun, British and French forces attacked on the Somme, a battle which lasted from June 26 to November 26 1916, in which, once more, the losses were enormous for little territorial gain.

In early 1917 the German Army suddenly withdrew to the prepared positions of the 'Siegfried Line', leaving a 'scorched earth' as they did so. On April 6 1917 came the news that the United States had entered the war, which was welcomed by Britain and France, but was followed by the French Army mutinies in May 1917, which were controlled only when General Petain took command.

In early 1918 the Germans staked all on a Spring offensive which achieved considerable initial successes but desperate measures by the Allies brought it to a halt. Then, in an astonishing change of role, the Allied armies, which had undergone four years of trench warfare followed by a defeat, went on the offensive and in a triumphant war of movement swept the Germans before them.

BELOW: Not all actions on the Western Front were fought from the trenches. Here two patrols have met in 'No Man's Land'; the Germans have gone to ground first and the French 'poilu' on the right has been hit and killed at very short range.

ABOVE: A German
machine-gun section
holding a barricade in
Poland. German-
Austrian forces were
held up by determined
Russian forces in 1915,
but were able to call on
reinforcements from the
Western Front.
Eventually, this,
combined with Russia's
terrible losses and
internal political chaos,
led to the disintegration
of the Russian Army in
1917.

Eastern Front

The war in the East began with a massive
struggle between Germany and Russia when,
as part of the France-Russian agreement, the
Russian forces pushed forward into East
Prussia, presenting the Germans with a second
front. The massive Russian armies were, however, badly commanded and poorly coordinated, and a Russian army was surrounded at the
Battle of Tannenburg (August 26-30 1914). In
the subsequent Battle of the Masurian Lakes
the offensive was effectively defeated and by
November both the German and Austro-
Hungarian armies were on the offensive.

In early 1916 the French appealed to their
Russian allies to launch another offensive to
ease the pressure on Verdun and the Russians,
under Brusilov, duly attacked, but lost many
men. Then the Italians appealed for pressure
on the Austro-Hungarians and General
Brusilov attacked in a successful, albeit costly,
operation which almost put Austria-Hungary
out of the war. This Russian advance was
eventually stopped by German reinforcements
rushed from the Verdun front.

Romania had been hesitant over joining the
war on the Allied side, but the early success of
the Brusilov offensive encouraged them to join
in, with disastrous consequences. Having
declared war on August 27 1916, by December
4 almost all of Romania had been conquered
by Germany and what was left of the
Romanian Army was sheltering in Russia.

The Russian Army's disastrous experiences,
coupled with long-standing political grievances
led to the outbreak of the Russian Revolution
on March 12 1917. The new government, led
by Kerensky, attempted to carry on fighting,
but discipline in both the army and navy broke
down, followed by widespread civil unrest and
culminating in the October Revolution. An
armistice was signed between Germany and
Russia's new government at Brest-Litovsk on
December 15 1917 and Russia was out of the
war, enabling German and Turkish troops to
be deployed to other fronts.

Dardanelles

One of the most controversial campaigns was
the Anglo-French assault on the Dardanelles,
which was intended to reopen the peacetime
sea route between Russia's Black Sea ports and
the West. This started as a naval operation, in
which the Turkish forts were shelled by Allied
battleships (February-March 1915) but the
ships withdrew after dense minefields were
encountered. An amphibious landing took
place on April 25, but the whole affair was
mismanaged and ended with the Allies in pos-
session of a number of small, narrow beach-
heads, all overlooked by Turkish forces. A second set of landings took place on August 6-8,
but also failed to achieve success. It was a
bloody, badly planned and poorly commanded
campaign, only redeemed by the bravery of the
soldiers on both sides. For the Allies, the only
real success was the withdrawal which took
place between November 23 and January 9

1916, which was brilliantly planned and executed.

Palestine

The British had occupied the Suez Canal Zone for many years and in December 1914 they declared Egypt to be a Protectorate. In January 1917 troops moved eastward from the Canal, clearing the Sinai Peninsula with little difficulty. They then pushed north, but were held during two assaults on Gaza, until the arrival of General Allenby. The third assault on Gaza was successful and on December 9 1917 the British rode into Jerusalem. Allenby's offensive was temporarily halted by the requirement to send troops to the Western front, but following a mid-year reinforcement he moved north again on September 18 1918 and in a major battle at Megiddo (September 19-21) he inflicted a massive defeat on the Turks and commenced a pursuit northwards. This quickly resulted in Turkish requests for an armistice, which was signed on October 30.

Italy

Italy declared war on Austria-Hungary (but not Germany) on May 23 1915 and commenced attacking on the Isonzo front the following month. A series of nine offensives on the Isonzo during 1915 and 1916 served little purpose other than to exhaust both sides and to inflict heavy casualties on both. In answer to an Austria-Hungarian appeal the Germans came to their support in October 1917, but in early 1918 the troops were transferred back to the Western Front, the Germans telling the Austria-Hungarians that, since Russia had been eliminated from the war, they should be able to deal with the Italians on their own. The Austria-Hungarians attacked in June 1918, but were held by the Allies (the Italians had now been joined by American, British and French troops). The Allies then began a major counterattack culminating in the Battle of Vittorio

Veneto (October 24-November 4), which resulted in massive Austria-Hungarian losses, and an armistice was then signed.

Other land campaigns

Germany had a number of colonies in Africa, Asia and the Pacific, most of which were impossible to defend and were quickly taken over by the Allies. The exception was German East Africa where the commander, von Lettow-Vorbeck, with a force numbering some 4,000 men, conducted a brilliant guerrilla campaign which started on the first day of the war and only ended when he was informed by the British that the Armistice had been signed in Europe.

Other campaigns were fought in the Caucasus, the Balkans, Persia, Salonika and Mesopotamia, but these were peripheral to the main campaigns which were on the Western and, to a lesser extent, Eastern fronts.

ABOVE: Emir Faisal and his bodyguard in the Arabian desert.

BELOW: A company of Askaris in German East Africa. Under the command of von Lettow-Vorbeck they evaded capture by much superior British forces until the end of the war.

ABOVE: A torpedo from a German U-boat strikes a halted and abandoned British merchant ship. The U-boats brought Britain closer to defeat than any other weapon.

The naval war

August 1914 found the massive British Grand Fleet in its war bases at Scapa Flow and the Firth of Forth, while the German High Seas Fleet was in the Jade river. The British had numerous ships in the Mediterranean, while there were ten German cruisers in the Atlantic and Pacific. 1914 saw two chilling foretastes of what was to come when the German submarine *U-9* sank three British cruisers in quick succession (September 22) and German heavy cruisers shelled British coastal towns (December 16). The British suffered a setback when two of their cruisers were sunk at the Battle of Coronel on November 1 1914, but the German ships were then themselves sunk off the Falkland Islands on December 8.

In 1915 a naval action off the Dogger Bank in the North Sea ended inconclusively while the Germans, finding the British maritime blockade ever more effective, unleashed the first submarine campaign. Numerous British ships were sunk, including the *Lusitania* and *Arabic*, both of which had American passengers aboard, and US diplomatic protests were so strong that the German government called off the campaign on September 1.

One of the two great naval episodes of the war was the Battle of Jutland on May 31-June 1 1916. Both the British and German navies had been spoiling for a major fight since the war began, and Jutland was hard fought on both sides. It began at about 1530 with an engagement between the battlecruiser forces, with the Germans (commanded by Hipper) seeking to draw the British (Beatty) down on to the main High Seas Fleet. Beatty lost two ships and then sighted the main German fleet (Scheer) at 1642

THE BATTLE OF JUTLAND

SHIP TYPE	ENGAGED		LOST	
	British	German	British	German
Batleships	28	22		1
Battlecruisers	9	5	3	1
Cruisers:				
armoured	8	0		
light	26	11	3	4
Destroyers:				
leaders	5	0		
destroyers	73	61	8	5
Minelayers	1	0		
Seaplane carriers	1	0		
TOTALS	**151**	**99**	**14**	**11**
MEN			**6,784**	**3,039**

ALLIED SHIPPING LOSSES TO U-BOATS 1914-18

	Number of ships	Gross registered tonnage
Aug-Dec 1914	3	2,950
1915	636	1,191,704
1916	1,309	2,186,462
1917	n.k.	6,149,070
Jan-Nov 1918	1,305	2,754,152
TOTALS	**3,253**	**12,284,338**

GERMAN U-BOAT GAINS/LOSSES 1914-18

	Start strength	U-Boat losses	Entered service	End strength
Aug-Dec 1914	28	5	11	34
1915	34	22	52	64
1916	64	23	108	149
1917	149	67	87	169
Jan-Nov 1918	169	86	88	171
TOTALS		**203**	**346**	

and turned north, as he was instructed to, in order to lure the Germans on to the guns of the Grand Fleet (Jellicoe). Just before 1830 the two main fleets engaged each other and with his fleet in a disadvantageous position, the German admiral, Scheer, made a simultaneous 180 degree turn away, followed by a second, similar turn at 1855. There were a number of engagements but the fighting faded away as night fell, with the British between the Germans and their bases. During the night, however, Scheer managed to get past the British.

For the British, nurtured in a tradition of naval excellence, this appeared to be a failure; the Germans had suffered fewer losses in both men and ships, and the remainder had escaped to fight another day. There were many reasons for the lack of British success, the main ones being communications problems and the weak protection of their battlecruisers. For the Germans, it was initially publicised as a success, but it demonstrated that the High Seas Fleet would never be able to defeat the British.

Meanwhile, the Germans concentrated on the submarine war and in February 1917 the second unrestricted campaign was instigated. The effect was almost catastrophic for the British, whose losses soared from 300,000 tons in December 1916 to 875,000 tons in May 1917. Finally, and despite considerable reluc-

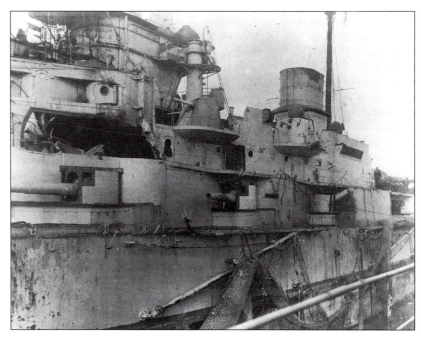

tance at high levels, the British introduced the convoy system and the losses immediately fell, while sinkings of U-boats increased.

The remainder of the war at sea passed relatively quietly. The British maintained their Grand Fleet at Scapa Flow, reinforced by a squadron of US Navy battleships in 1917 and a second in 1918. There were a number of small operations, including German destroyer raids into the English Channel and a British raid on the U-boat bases at Ostende

ABOVE: German battle-cruiser *Derfflinger* after the Battle of Jutland. This battle proved to the Germans that they would never win a surface conflict, so they switched to U-boats, instead.

LEFT: Seamen cling to the hull of German armoured cruiser *Blücher* which was sunk during the Battle of Dogger Bank, January 24 1915. She was hit first by British battlecruiser HMS *Lion*, then finished off by four others as a result of a communication mix-up, during which three other German battlecruisers, plus several other vessels, were allowed to escape.

ABOVE: A propaganda picture depicting a German U-boat halting an American merchant-ship. It was such attacks which eventually drew the United States into the war.

Zeebrugge. One massive operation involved laying a mine barrier across the northern end of the North Sea in an attempt to prevent U-boats escaping into the Atlantic. An Anglo-American force laid the mines between March and October 1918, four British ships laying 15,093 mines and ten US ships 56,033 mines. The mine barrier was completed, but whether it was worth the effort involved was the subject of much debate in the inter-war years. Finally, the crews of the German High Seas Fleet mutinied on October 29 1918 and then, following the Armistice, the once-proud fleet sailed into internment on November 21.

The naval war in the Mediterranean started with the German battlecruiser *Goeben* escaping from the British and reaching Turkey, where it became *Yavuz*. The Anglo-French fleet main operations were in support of the armies in the operations in the Dardanelles and in blockading the Austria-Hungarian fleet in the Adriatic. The U-boat war was also intense and the two highest scoring 'aces' both operated there. The German ace was Lothar von Arnauld de la Perriere, who sank 189 merchant ships (446,708 tons) and three warships, while the Austrian ace was Ritter von Trapp who sank one warship, one submarine and 12 merchantmen (45,668 tons).

The air war
Although not the first in which aircraft actually took part, the First World War was certainly the first in which aircraft played a significant role. Initially, aircraft were used for reconnaissance and artillery 'spotting' – as were dirigibles and balloons – and they were countered by ground artillery and small arms fire, but it quickly became clear that the best anti-aircraft system to use was another aircraft. At first, the

weapons were rudimentary 'darts dropped from one aircraft on to another and pistols or rifles wielded by the crew – but soon machine-guns were in use and the fighter was born.

WWI ESTIMATED LOSSES ENTENTE POWERS (millions)

COUNTRY	Total forces	Military dead	Military wounded
Belgium	2.67	0.13	0.45
British Empire	8.90	0.90	2.10
France	8.41	1.36	4.27
Greece	0.23	0.05	0.21
Italy	5.62	0.46	0.95
Japan	0.80	0.003	0.09
Montenegro	0.05	0.03	0.10
Portugal	0.10	0.07	0.13
Romania	0.75	0.34	0.12
Russia	12.00	1.70	4.95
USA	4.36	0.05	0.21
TOTALS	**43.89**	**5.55**	**13.58**

WWI ESTIMATED LOSSES CENTRAL POWERS (millions)

COUNTRY	Total forces	Military dead	Military wounded
Austria-Hungary	7.80	0.92	0.92
Bulgaria	1.20	0.75	0.15
Germany	11.0	1.81	4.25
Turkey	2.85	0.33	0.40
TOTALS	**22.85**	**3.81**	**5.72**

Strategic bombing also saw its genesis with Zeppelins carrying out their first raids on England in January 1915, with a mass attack on London in October 1915. These continued in 1916, but it was not until September that any were shot down, one by an aircraft and two by ground gunfire.

One of the most significant events of the air war was administrative rather than tactical, when the British removed the aviation elements from the Army and Navy and fused them to form a totally new service, the Royal Air Force, equal in status to the other two traditional services. This took place in April 1918 and was an example later followed in the armed forces of almost every country in the world.

ABOVE: A remarkable picture of the first Zeppelin raid on London in 1915. There were 19 raids during the year and at first the British had no defences at all.

BELOW: British De Havilland DH.2 fighter in 1916. It had a pusher propeller so that the machine-gun could be mounted in the nose.

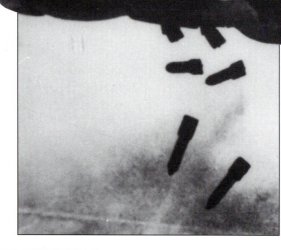

RIGHT: German Heinkel He 111 bomber dropping bombs over London during the 'Blitz'.

BELOW: British soldiers wade out to a rescue ship off Dunkirk, while others patiently await their turn on the shore.

Second World War 1939-1945

The Second World War lasted from September 1 1939, when German troops crossed the border into Poland, until September 2 1945, when the formal Japanese surrender was signed in Tokyo Bay. It is impossible to give precise figures, but during that time some 100 million men bore arms, of which 15 million died. Not only was it the greatest military conflict, but it also involved civilian populations in an unprecedented manner, with approximately 30 million deaths, of which some 6 million Jews and 4 million Poles were deliberately exterminated by Nazi killers. It ended with the explosion of two atomic bombs, the weapon which has subsequently dominated all military and political planning and conduct.

Like the First World War, the Second was inevitable, but for a different reason. Under the Nazis, Germany expanded rapidly and on each occasion the international community failed to react sternly. Thus, Germany reoccupied the Rhineland in 1936, invaded and took over Austria in March 1938, was given the Sudetenland under the Munich Agreement (September 1938), and annexed Bohemia-Moravia and Memel (both in March 1939). Convinced that he was immune to international reaction, Hitler invaded Poland and only then did France and Great Britain react and, when Hitler failed to reply to their ultimatum, go to war. Italy joined the war in part because Mussolini shared the same fascist ideology, but also to achieve national political expansionist aims.

Like Germany, Japan had expanded its territories in the 1930s and was not strongly opposed by any of the other major powers. Considering itself threatened in 1941 it went to war with the USA, the British Empire and the Dutch. There was some cooperation between the Germans and the Japanese, but what little help they were able to give each other made no difference whatsoever to their respective war efforts.

The European war – land

Initial moves – German forces crossed the Polish border on the morning of September 1 1939: 1,250,000 men in 9 armored and 51 infantry divisions. In a lightning campaign the Polish forces were overwhelmed, surrendering on October 25, and there was then a lengthy lull before Germany struck again. This time Germany took Denmark in a virtually blood-less attack on April 9 1940 and invaded Norway. British and French troops reinforced Norway but the German victory was not long delayed and the Allies withdrew on June 7-9 1940. Mcanwhile, the Germans attacked in the West on May 10, passing, as in the First World War, through Belgium, and the British Expeditionary Force was driven back into Dunkirk, from which the majority of the force was evacuated to England between May 28 and June 4. It took the Germans just three more weeks to finish off the campaign, with the French being forced to capitulate on June 21 in a ceremony held in the railway coach where the Germans had signed the Armistice in 1918. In just a few weeks Hitler had achieved the victory in the West that had eluded the Imperial German Army for four years between 1914 and 1918. In a sad post-script to the campaign the British sank most of the French fleet in Oran harbor, having first offered the choice of sailing to England or scut-tling the ships where they were; it was to embitter Anglo-French relations for years.

The British were now the only power resisting the German advance in Western Europe and the *Luftwaffe* (air force) attempted to sub-due the country by means of a concentrated bombing campaign. The 'Battle of Britain' last-ed from August 8 to October 30 1940 as the *Luftwaffe* sought to achieve the air superiority which would enable an invasion (Operation Sea Lion) to take place. The battle swayed to and fro, but British radar and a highly effective ground control system enabled the relatively small force, composed primarily of the excel-lent Hurricane and Spitfire fighters, to be used to maximum effect: 1,733 German aircraft were shot down compared to 915 British. Although the attempt to subdue the Royal Air Force had failed, fierce bombing attacks on British cities, especially London and Coventry, continued in a campaign known to the British as 'the blitz'.

North Africa

For some years Italy had been expanding its colonies on Africa, and its leader Mussolini had developed an ambitious plan to cut the British Empire's lifeline through the Mediter-ranean by attacking the Suez Canal. British commander, General Wavell, with his head-quarters in Cairo, Egypt, was faced by numer-ous threats: Italians in Libya, Ethiopia and Somaliland; Vichy French in Syria; fascists in Iraq; and Germans invading Greece.

On September 13 1940, after much prod-

BELOW: Assessing the damage at dawn on London's East End: September 25 1940

BOTTOM: The fighting in the Western Desert was conducted in a hard but chivalrous manner. Here, two Australians help a wounded German to the field dressing station.

BELOW: Rommel (with hat) and staff officers. A charismatic general, Rommel was respected by both sides in the Desert War.

ding from Rome, the Italian Army in Libya advanced a short distance into Egypt and then halted. General Wavell had many other strategic commitments and it was not until December 9 that he was able to launch a counterattack. This exceeded beyond all expectations, driving the Italians 500 miles (800km) back into Cyrenaica where a large force surrendered to a much smaller British force at Beda Fomm.

Concurrently with this campaign, Wavell launched an invasion of Ethiopia and Somaliland in which the Italians again fared badly, culminating in the return of Emperor Haile Selassie to Addis Ababa on April 4 1941. Meanwhile, the Germans were about to come to the aid of their Italian allies, whose Balkan campaign had bogged down, and Wavell was ordered to send troops to Greece. The British arrived in late March and the Germans invaded on April 9; their advance was so rapid that the Greeks surrendered on April 23 and the British, after heavy losses, withdrew on April 27. Part of the British force was redeployed to Crete, which was attacked by German paratroops on May 20. A fiercely fought battle resulted in yet another British withdrawal, although the losses among the German paratroops were so heavy that Hitler never again used them in the parachute assault role.

Back in the Western desert the poor performance by Italian troops spurred Hitler to send a small force, the *Deutsches Afrika Korps* commanded by the previously little-known Major-General Rommel, to help his allies in Cyrenaica. There then followed a 'see-saw' campaign, in which the two sides took it in

turn to push the other backwards, until the attackers' supply lines were stretched to breaking point, while the defender was on top of his own base and able to launch a counter-attack, whereupon the cycle repeated itself. Rommel swept straight on to the offensive, driving the British back and laying siege to a hastily assembled garrison in Tobruk. Wavell was replaced by Auchinleck on July 1 and a new British operation in November/December achieved some success, including raising the siege of Tobruk. Rommel's second offensive began on January 21, but the British stood at Gazala from February to June, when a renewed German attack pushed them back into Egypt to the Alamein line. The Germans also took Tobruk in a quick attack, which dealt a severe blow to British morale.

At this point Lieutenant-General Montgomery was appointed commander of 8th Army and he parried Rommel's next attack (Battle of Alam Halfa). He continued to prepare for his own attack, in which he was determined that his troops would have every advantage and that this time there would be no more 'see-sawing'. The Battle of El Alamein lasted from October 23 to November 4 and was by no means all plain sailing, but at the end the Axis forces were utterly beaten, having lost 34,000 Germans and 25,000 Italians killed, wounded and captured, against 13,000 British; losses in tanks, artillery and other equipment were in similar proportions.

Montgomery was determined that this time there would be no mistake and his pursuit of Rommel's forces was methodical rather than dashing. Rommel was also particularly adept at escaping from traps, but it made little differ-ence and the 8th Army pressed on inexorably, pushing the Axis forces back towards Tunisia.

Operation Torch

Meanwhile, the US and the UK were invading the other end of the North African littoral in Operation Torch. This first Allied invasion went remarkably well, despite its complexity. There were three elements: Western Task Force (under General Patton) sailed from the USA to attack Casablanca; Central Task Force (Fredendall) sailed from England for Oran; and Eastern Task Force (Ryder) also sailed from England to land at Algiers. The landings started on November 8 and complete surprise was achieved. French forces on the spot put up some resistance and then surrendered, although the Vichy regime in Metropolitan France supported German resistance to the invasion.

Progress was not all easy, however, with strong German resistance slowing down the Allied advance. There was a setback at the Battle of Kasserine, but eventually the Allies reached Tunis and on May 11 1943 it was all over and the Axis had been expelled from Africa.

Sicily and Italy

Allied planning for the invasion of Sicily had begun long before Tunis was captured and the Anglo-American landing took place on July 9 1943, with the US 7th Army (Patton) on the left and the British 8th Army (Montgomery) on the right. The Allies were in Messina by August 17, although the Germans managed to pass rather more over to Italy than had been hoped.

The Italian people deposed Mussolini on July 24 and the new leader, Badoglio, conclud-

ABOVE: German paratroops advancing during the attack on Crete, an operation that was so costly that Hitler never permitted another major airborne operation.

ABOVE: US infantry storm ashore from a US Coast Guard landing craft onto a Normandy beach. Although the Germans were expecting an Allied invasion, the actual event achieved complete tactical surprise.

BELOW: American paratroops continue to advance under German artillery fire in an attack near Arnhem in the Netherlands in October 1944.

ed an armistice with the Allies which became effective on September 8 1943, five days after the first Allied landing on mainland Italy. The main landing was at Salerno on September 9, which almost turned into a disaster as one of the most skilful of German commanders, Kesselring, mounted a counter-attack which very nearly drove the invaders back into the sea. Allied strength, coupled with command of the air and sea, eventually predominated, and Kesselring disengaged and withdrew northward.

For the remainder of the war the Allies fought their way up the Italian peninsula. The Anzio landing on January 22 1944 was supposed to expedite the process but, like the Salerno landing, very nearly came unstuck. The Germans under Kesselring proved masterly in defence, nowhere more so than at Monte Cassino which resisted from February 12 to May 18. Rome was taken on June 4 and by the

end of the year the Allies had closed up to the Gothic line.

D-Day and NW Europe

The British planning for a cross-Channel invasion began almost directly after Dunkirk, with the Americans becoming involved as soon as they joined the war. The operation was the overall responsibility of the Supreme Headquarters Allied Expeditionary Forces (SHAEF), commanded by General Eisenhower, with the overall command of the landing being the responsibility of General Montgomery.

After a 24 hour delay due to bad weather, the operation started just after midnight on June 4 1944 with parachute and glider landings to secure key points, followed by the first wave of amphibious landings at first light. Despite the fact that the Germans had been waiting for months for an invasion, it achieved total tactical surprise. It was the largest and most complicated amphibious operation ever undertaken, involving well over a million men, tens of thousands of aircraft and thousands of ships, and went remarkably well, helped considerably by the Allied mastery of the sea and air.

By the first night the Allies were securely ashore and began to push the Germans slowly back. Montgomery sought to attract the German reserves to the British position on the Allied left to free the Americans, first to take the Cherbourg peninsula and then to break out. Success came in early August with Patton's Third Army making the crucial break out, following which the German position collapsed

Airborne Divisions were successful but the third, by the British 1st Airborne Division was a gallant failure. Despite this set-back the Allied advance continued on a front stretching from the Swiss border to the North Sea.

Suddenly, the Germans struck back in the Ardennes, intending to split the Allied forces into two, drive through to the sea at Antwerp and then eliminate the forces to the north of the salient. A dense blanket of fog, rain and snow grounded Allied aircraft and prevented them detecting the assembly of 41 divisions (14 of them panzer divisions) and the Germans achieved both strategic and tactical surprise, penetrating deep into Allied territory. The Allies, however, showed remarkable flexibility, with Montgomery taking command of all forces north of 'The Bulge' while Patton's Third Army swung through 90 degrees to operate northwards against the Germans' southern flank. Heroic defense at Bastogne, coupled with pressure all around the perimeter first halted and then turned back the German operation and the Allied advance then continued up to the Rhine.

The Allied crossings of the Rhine took dif-

and the Allies were soon in full pursuit, with Paris being liberated on August 5 1944.

A second landing, Operation Dragoon, took place on August 15 in the south of France. The landing was a success, the bridgehead expanded rapidly and the US Seventh Army drove northwards, joining up with Patton's Third Army on September 11.

By September the Allies were approaching the German frontiers and in an attempt to speed the process a major parachute operation was conducted by First Allied Airborne Army. The aim was to seize three bridge to enable the British to swing around the upper end of the Siegfried Line and roll it up from the North. The first two drops by the US 101st and 82nd

ferent forms. In the centre an American task force reached the bridge at Remagen on March 7 to find it still standing and only lightly defended, and in a brilliant operation captured it before the defenders could blow it. First Army quickly seized the opportunity and established a bridgehead from which German counter-attacks were unable to shift them. In the South Patton crossed at Oppenheim on March 22, an operation with neither air nor artillery build-up which took the Germans completely by surprise. In the North a set-piece attack was mounted on March 23, and within three days there were 12 bridges across the river, and the Western Allies were advancing again towards their junction with the Russians.

ABOVE: The relaxed stances of these Americans on Utah beach on D-Day, June 6 1944, show that the morning's heavy fighting is over, but a mortar crew continues to fire against a German target.

largest single attack in history up to that time and German estimates were that the campaign would last approximately four months. Minsk and Smolensk were taken in mid-July, followed by Kiev on September 19. By November the German armies were in sight of Moscow and the Soviet government had moved eastward to Kuibyshev. The successes were stunning but, on the other hand, the Red Army was deliberately trading space for time, and despite tremendous losses was by no means beaten. The first Soviet counter-offensive began in December 1941 and at one time threatened to inflict disaster on the German army, but the Germans withstood the triple enemy of Russia, snow and mud, and endured through to Spring, when they once again went on the offensive.

Sebastopol was captured on July 2, leading to a drive towards the Caucasus, but Hitler's attention then veered to Stalingrad, a name that was to become engrained in German con-

ABOVE: A German flame-thrower crew at work during the invasion of the Soviet Union, Operation Barbarossa.

RIGHT: A German demolition squad in the town of Zhitomer, shortly before it was recaptured by the advancing Red Army. The death and destruction in Eastern Europe was far greater than anything experienced in the West.

Eastern Europe

The USSR and Germany had supported opposite sides in the Spanish Civil War (1936-39) and in the Czech crisis (1938), but this was suddenly reversed with the signing of the Non-Aggression pact with Germany on August 27 1939. This enabled the Soviets to attack Poland, which was partitioned with Germany, on September 17, thereafter attacking Finland on November 30 1939, occupying Estonia, Latvia and Lithuania on June 15 1940. They also protected their rear by signing a Non-Aggression Treaty with Japan on April 13 1941.

Despite a variety of warning signals, the German attack on June 22 1941 (Operation Barbarossa) took the Soviet armed forces and leadership by surprise. The attack involved some 3 million men in 162 divisions, the

sciousness. The Red Army (commanded by Zhukov) surrounded the German Sixth Army (von Paulus) and, despite desperate efforts to relieve the beleaguered garrison, Hitler's order to resist at all costs led to the loss the entire army; originally 300,000 strong, some 92,000 survived to go into captivity.

On July 5 1943 there began the Battle of Kursk, which is still the largest single armour battle in history. The Germans lost some 3,000 tanks, 70,000 men killed or wounded, 1,000 guns, 5,000 trucks and some 1,400 aircraft, while Soviet losses were probably slightly less. Soviet pressure increased throughout the remainder of the year, while Hitler's attention was diverted to the Allied invasion of Sicily and Italy, the loss of Italy as an ally, and the impending invasion of France.

By early 1944 the Soviets were on the

advance everywhere and by July they had crossed the Polish border. A large German force was pinned into the Crimea, but managed to escape by sea (April/May 1944). The Second World War was generally a very unpleasant conflict, but in one of the more cynical moves the Soviets halted their advance through Poland while the German SS subdued the Warsaw Uprising between August 1 and September 30. Romania fell to the Red Army in September, Bulgaria changed sides on September 8. By January 12 1945 the Red Army was across the German border, with the northern elements on the Baltic coast, while in the South the Russians were storming along the Danube Valley. The Germans were now short of equipment, short of men, but, perhaps most importantly, they were running out of fuel.

To the Red Army fell the honour of taking the enemy capital, Berlin, which fell on May 2. Unfortunately, Hitler, the evil genius who, more than any other single individual, was responsible for the five years of bloodshed in Europe, had committed suicide on April 30.

The European war – sea

The outbreak of war found the British and French fleets combined, while the German and Italian navies, although sizeable, were unable to cooperate. Meanwhile in the South Atlantic the 'pocket battleship' Graf Spee was at large sinking numerous merchant ships. It required

the British and French to deploy large forces to look for her. Three British cruisers met Graf Spee on December 13 1939 and after a sharp engagement in which one British ship, Exeter, was seriously damaged, the German captain (Langsdorff) headed for nearby Montevideo to effect repairs. Forced to leave the port after 72 hours, Langsdorff blew up his ship in international waters, and he and his crew then sought refuge in nearby Argentina. Having ensured the safety of his crew, Langsdorff committed suicide, but the episode drew criticism from Hitler and thereafter German ships fought to the last round.

ABOVE: The capture of the Nazi capital of Berlin is marked by a Russian sergeant erecting the 'Hammer and Sickle' over the Reichstag on May 2 1945.

FLEET STRENGTHS ON ENTRY TO WORLD WAR TWO[1]

	Entered war: August 1939				Entered war: 22 June 1941[2]	Entered war: December 1941	
	UK[3]	France	Germany[4]	Italy	USSR	USA[5]	Japan
Battleships, Battlecruisers[6]	18	11	4	6	3	17	11[7]
Aircraft carriers	10	1	1	–	–	7	11
Cruisers	77	50	13[8]	47	7	54	41
Destroyers	205	34	25	59	54	173	129
Submarines	70	72	98	115	210	112	67

[1] Figures include ships on the verge of completion.

[2] The Soviet Navy was split between the Arctic, Baltic, Black Sea and Pacific Fleets.

[3] At this time the British Royal Navy included all (then) Empire elements, including Australia, Canada, India, New Zealand, etc. Note also that the British fleet was deployed around the world and was not confined to European waters.

[4] The German Navy consisted almost entirely of very modern ships.

[5] On entry into the war the US fleet was split approximately 50:50 between the Pacific and Atlantic Oceans.

[6] Battlecruisers were the same size and had the same armament as battleships but were faster, which was acheived by having reduced armour protection.

[7] Included Yamato, the largest battleship built to that date; a second and slightly larger sistership was completed in 1942.

[8] Includes three so-called 'pocket battleships' which were actually heavy cruisers (and were called 'panzerschiffe' by the German Navy).

ABOVE: A desperate
scene as survivors of
the German battleship
Bismarck wait to be
hoisted aboard a British
warship on May 28
1941.

Other commerce raiding operations were
undertaken by *Admiral Scheer*, by the battlecruisers *Gneisenau* and *Scharnhorst* acting
together, and, separately, by cruisers *Hipper*
and *Prinz Eugen*. Other operations were
undertaken by converted merchantmen, such
as *Pinguin*, but this all finished in 1944.

The cruise of the battleship *Bismarck* was
intended to be the greatest commerce attack of
all, when it sortied from Germany in company
with *Prinz Eugen* in May 1941. The two ships
met the British battlecruiser *Hood* and battleship *Prince of Wales* in the Denmark Strait; in
a very brief engagement *Hood* was sunk and
Prince of Wales damaged. *Bismarck* continued
into the Atlantic but its steering was damaged
by an air-launched torpedo and it was eventually brought to battle and sunk with heavy loss
of life on May 28.

Hitler ordered that *Scharnhorst, Gneisenau*
and *Prinz Eugen* be brought home from Brest
to Germany, and that they were to be routed
up the English Channel. This duly took place
on February 11-13 and was a great success; the
British were anticipating such an operation but
even so were taken completely by surprise.
While in Kiel *Gneisenau* was so badly damaged in a bombing raid that it was stripped of

its guns, while *Prinz Eugen* , although remaining operational until the end of the war, was
never again employed outside the Baltic.
Scharnhorst, however, was sent to Norway in
March 1943, where it eventually sailed against
a Scotland-Murmansk convoy on December 25
1943. It was sunk by the British on December
26. As with *Bismarck*, *Scharnhorst* fought to
the last round, with only 36 of its 1,900 crew
surviving.

Tirpitz, sister ship of the ill-fated *Bismarck*,
spent virtually its entire career in Norwegian
fjords, posing a constant threat to convoys running to Murmansk. It made only one sortie of
any importance, when, in company with
Scharnhorst, it attacked a coal-mining installa-
tion on Spitzbergen, although this was hardly a
fitting mission for such a mighty ship. The ship
was attacked several times by the British,
including midget submarines (September
1943), carrier-borne aircraft (April 3 1944)
and twice by RAF bombers, one on September
15 and finally on November 12 1944, when
she sank with much loss of life. The German
Navy's surface war was over.

The U-boat war

The German Navy's most effective weapon
was, however, the U-boat. *U-30* sank the liner
Athenia on the day war broke out, *U-29* sank
the carrier *Courageous* on September 17th, and
U-47 sank the battleship *Royal Oak* in the
strongly protected base at Scapa Flow on
October 14. Unlike in the First World War the
British Admiralty immediately implemented
convoys and, realising that escorts would be
needed in large numbers, the British obtained
50 elderly destroyers from the USA in exchange
for leases on bases in Newfoundland, the West
Indies and Central America. Even so, 147 ships
(500,000 tons) were sunk in the first four
months of war, rising to well over two million
tons in 1940 and 1941. The Germans introduced the 'wolf pack' concept in which a long
line of U-boats spread across selected areas of
the Atlantic and as soon as one had a sighting it

THE U-BOAT WAR 1939-45

	Start strength	U-Boat losses	Entered service	End strength
Sep-Dec 1939	57	9	6	54
1940	54	25	54	83
1941	83	35	202	250
1942	250	85	238	403
1943	403	241	290	452
1944	452	254	230	428
Jan-May 1945	428	172	93	349
TOTALS		**821**	**1,113**	

ALLIED SHIPPING LOSSES TO U-BOATS 1939-45

	Number of ships	Gross registered tonnage
Sep-Dec 1939	147	509,321
1940	520	2,462,867
1941	458	2,300,689
1942	1,155	6,149,473
1943	457	2,536,757
1944	127	672,338
Jan-May 1945	63	284,476
TOTALS	**2,927**	**14,915,921**

LEFT: German battleship *Tirpitz* in Kaafjord, Norway; a very detailed picture taken by an RAF photo-recce aircraft in July 1944, after attacks by Royal Navy midget submarines in September 1943 and Fleet Air Arm bombers in April 1944.

started shadowing the convoy and radioed to the others in the group to join it. The U-boat campaign was helped by two other factors: the unexpected bonus of the French Atlantic ports which fell into German Navy hands saving the time-consuming long haul around the British Isles; and breaking the British and Allied Merchant Ship (BAMS) code.

The British had two weapons not available in 1918. Sonar (sound *n*avigation *a*nd *r*anging), which was known to the British as Asdic,

was a substantial improvement in searching techniques. The other weapon was the aircraft and this did prove highly effective. Land-based aircraft with ever longer range were deployed and escort carriers were designed and built to enable ASW aircraft to go to sea with the ships they were protecting.

As soon as Germany and Italy declared war on the USA (December 11 1941), U-boats headed for the eastern coast in an operation officially designated *Paukenschlag* (= drum beat) but unofficially known as 'the happy time' where they found lighthouses still working, coastal towns lit up and ships with lights shining, proceeding as they had in peacetime. The Allied ASW effort was then dramatically affected by the German introduction of an upgraded version of the Enigma code-breaking machine with a fourth rotor, which included a new system for fewer and shorter signals. This removed at a stroke the U-boat information which was beginning to enable the Allies to master the situation, and it took many months before British Ultra decoders had restored the situation to its previous level. By late 1942, however, the balance in the Battle of the Atlantic was starting to shift; 85 U-boats had been sunk, but while Allied losses were still

LEFT: German battleship *Bismarck* fires a broad-side at British battle-ship *Prince of Wales*, May 21 1941. This German picture was taken from *Bismarck*'s escorting cruiser *Prinz Eugen*.

ABOVE: A German crew carefully loading a 21 inch (533mm) torpedo aboard their Type VIIC U-boat. The weapon in the foreground is a water-proofed version of the famous 88mm AA gun.

very considerable US production of both naval and merchant vessels was rising rapidly.

In January 1943 Admiral Dönitz took over as head of the German Navy and the U-boat war intensified, reaching its peak in April/May 1943 with two separate events. In the first, Convoy ONS-2, consisting of 42 merchant ships, fought its way across the Atlantic, coming under attack from no fewer than 51 U-boats. The U-boats sank 13 ships, but lost five of their own to the convoy escorts and another two to aircraft. Also in May airborne microwave radar became operational in ASW aircraft, making life even more difficult for U-boats, especially in the Bay of Biscay.

Then, in June, hunter/killer groups consisting of an escort carrier and a number of destroyers were introduced and, using a combination of normal and Ultra intelligence, they were able to achieve considerable success against the U-boats, especially in eliminating the supply boats (Milchcows). The Germans brought new devices into operation such as

radar detectors, increased AA guns, schnorkel tubes which enabled U-boats to remain submerged while recharging their batteries, and even totally new designs of much faster submarines, but they failed to break the Allied dominance of the Atlantic. Their difficulties were exacerbated by the loss of the French ports in June 1944. The Allies had won the Battle of the Atlantic.

The Mediterranean

At the start of the war the Italian fleet was, at least on paper, both strong and modern, and posed a major threat to the British in the Mediterranean. A significant blow was, however, dealt on November 11 1940 when 21 Swordfish biplanes attacked the Italian fleet in harbor at Taranto and severely damaged three battleships, two cruisers and two auxiliaries, a demonstration of air power which foreshadowed Pearl Harbor, but seems to have gone unremarked at the time.

The next year saw the only British major fleet action of the European war, off Cape Matapan, when the Italians put to sea on March 26 with three battleships, eight cruisers and 13 destroyers, intending to attack British convoys to Greece. Radio messages decrypted in Britain indicated an operation near Crete and the British Mediterranean Fleet sailed with three battleships, one aircraft carrier, four cruisers and 13 destroyers. The Italian ships were located by *Formidable*'s aircraft at about midday on March 28 and carried out torpedo attacks on the battleship *Vittorio Veneto* and the cruiser *Pola*, the latter being badly dam-

lost in the Greek operation, followed by two cruisers and another destroyer off Crete, with two battleships and two more cruisers seriously damaged. The only consolation for the British was that they located a German attempt to send troops to Crete using a miscellany of small craft, numbers of which were sunk with heavy loss of life.

The end of 1941 was a particularly bad month for the British Mediterranean Fleet. The battleship *Barham* was sunk by U-331 on November 25, while on the morning of December 19 three British cruisers and four destroyers blundered into an Italian minefield; one cruiser and the destroyer were sunk and the other two cruisers damaged. That night, in one of the most distinguished small operations of the war, three Italian human torpedoes, each manned by two men, penetrated the defences of Alexandria harbour and severely damaged two battleships, putting them out of service for many months.

The European war – air

The Second World War started with two devastating demonstrations of air power by the Germans, first in the campaign in Poland and second in the campaign in France. In both, the *Luftwaffe* was employed in support of the army in so-called *blitzkrieg* offensives, where fighters fought for and obtained air supremacy, while light bombers and, in particular, dive-bombers, were available at very short notice to give pin-point support whenever the ground troops were held up. This worked with devastating efficiency in these two campaigns, tending to obscure the fact that the concept depended upon air supremacy and as soon as that was challenged the bombers, and in particular the Ju-87 Stuka, was very vulnerable.

aged and brought to a stop. In the evening part of the Italian fleet returned to recover *Pola* only to meet the British fleet. In a furious night action two cruisers and two destroyers were sunk and the abandoned *Pola* was finished off.

This effectively finished the Italian surface fleet as an effective force for the remainder of the war. In April, however, the British fleet was to suffer in its turn, when it evacuated British troops first from Greece and later from Crete, both under total German air superiority. Two destroyers and numerous smaller vessels were

LEFT: German Type VII U-boats return to their Norwegian base after their successful attacks on Allied Convoy PQ-17.

BELOW: Type VIIC U-boats surrendered at Wilhelmshaven in 1945. Type VIICs bore the lion's share of Germany's U-boat war, with 675 VIICs and VIIC-41s being commissioned, greater in number, by far, than any other type in submarine history.

ABOVE: A German Focke-Wulf FW-190 fighter turns under a pair of USAAF North American B-25 Mitchell medium bombers. The USAAF concentrated on daylight raids, while the British RAF Bomber Command attacked at night.

RIGHT: The cost to the USAAF was very high. Here a complete wing has been severed from a B-17 over Oranienburg, north of Berlin, on April 10 1945, just a few weeks before the war's end.

The first major confrontation came in the Battle of Britain (1940) when the *Luftwaffe* sought to achieve the air supremacy necessary for the invasion (Operation Sealion). At the start, *Luftwaffe* strength was approximately 900 fighters and 1,300 medium and light bombers, while the RAF could field 650 fighters. But the RAF had the inestimable advantage of radar to detect incoming aircraft and an extremely effective fighter control system, which, in combination, enabled the commander-in-chief, Air Chief Marshal Dowding, to achieve concentration of force where it was needed. In general, the battle consisted of:

July 10 – August 7 1940. Preliminary phase.
August 8 – 18. The start of the all-out aerial onslaught on Great Britain.
August 19 – September 5. The peak of the fighter combats, with the Luftwaffe concentrating on attacking RAF airfields.
September 6 – October 5. The height of the battle with the *Luftwaffe* switching its attack to London, peaking on September 15 and the last daylight raid on September 30.
October 6 – October 31. German fighters serving as fighter-bombers, with most raids being 'hit-and-run'.

At the time both sides greatly overestimated their scores, but post-war analysis suggests that the actual scores during the battle were: *Luftwaffe* losses 1,733 and RAF losses 915. In any event, the British had won and the

Luftwaffe switched its attention to the forthcoming Russian campaign.

The British bombing campaign had started in 1939 and slowly gathered pace with the first air raid on Berlin on August 24 1940, followed by two more on August 28 and 29. As Bomber Command expanded so the number and weight of attacks increased, although the accuracy was much less than had been anticipated in peacetime. The first firestorms were generated during a series of raids on Hamburg between July 26-29 1943, with a different type of raid on August 17/18, when the German rocket research and construction site at Peenemünde was attacked.

With the entry of America into the war the bombing effort was supplemented by the United States Army Air Force (USAAF), whose aircraft specialised in daylight raids, while RAF Bomber Command generally flew at night. The oil fields at Ploesti, Romania, were attacked in daring low-level air raids on August 1 1943, and Schweinfurt on October 14, but both raids were costly: 54 out of 178 were lost against Ploesti and 62 out of 328 against Schweinfurt. The pressure on Germany continued into 1944 until the strategic bombers were diverted briefly to tasks in preparation for D-Day, when targets in the general area of the forthcoming invasion were neutralised. The Allied aircraft were, however, switched back to the campaign in Germany once the invasion was safely under way.

One of the more controversial air raids was against Dresden on February 13-14 1945, when a very heavy RAF night raid was followed by a daylight USAAF raid. Damage was

extremely heavy, a large firestorm was generated and casualties were considerable. The bombing offensive ended on April 6 1945.

The Germans sought to redress the imbalance in the West with *Vergeltungswaffen* (*vergeltung* = vengeance) weapons, of which the only two to enter service were the V-1, a ramjet-powered, pilotless bomb, and the V-2, a large rocket. Both weapons were initially tar-

getted on London (although some were later launched at other targets in Great Britain), but the greatest numbers were, in fact, launched against targets in Belgium. Various countermeasures were used against the V-1 and in Great Britain 3,987 were destroyed, of which anti-aircraft guns accounted for 1,878, fighters for 1,847, and balloons for 232. There was no defence against the V-2 rocket.

ABOVE: The night belonged to RAF Bomber Command. Here an RAF Avro Lancaster heavy bomber is silhouetted over Hamburg on January 30 1943, with fire and flak painting crazy patterns below it.

V WEAPONS

	V-1 landed	V-2 landed	People killed	People wounded	Houses destroyed
British targets June 22 1944 – March 28 1945[1]	5,822	1,054	8,938	24,504	31,600
Belgian targets September 15 1944 – March 30 1945[2]	6,016	1,712	6,448	22,524	5,682
TOTALS	**11,837**	**2,764**	**15,386**	**47,028**	**37,282**

[1] Although London was the primary target for both V-1s and V-2s, more actually fell outside London than inside.
[2] Main targets in Belgium were Antwerp and its suburbs, Liege and Brussels.

ABOVE: US battleship *Arizona* (BB-39) blows up after the surprise Japanese attack on Pearl Harbor in the early morning of Sunday December 7 1941.

RIGHT: Japanese troops celebrate one of their many victories in the first two years of the Pacific War, this time on Bataan in the Philippines in 1942. There were only two such years, however, and then there was a rapid slide into defeat.

The Far Eastern war

The war between the Allies and Japan can best be split into two: the Pacific campaign between Japan and the USA, which also involved forces from Australia and New Zealand and, to a lesser extent, from the UK; and the war between Japan and the UK, which also involved China and the Netherlands in South-East Asia. The latter campaign involved both land and sea elements, which are treated separately, but in the campaign in the Pacific the ground and naval forces were so closely involved in the 'island-hopping' strategy that they must be treated together.

The war started on the morning of Sunday December 7 1941 with 360 Japanese naval aircraft attacking the US Pacific Fleet in Pearl Harbor. They inflicted considerable damage: four US battleships were destroyed and four seriously damaged, three cruisers and three destroyers were sunk; 261 aircraft were destroyed; and some 3,300 people killed and 1,400 wounded. It could have been much worse because, by chance, the most important ships, three aircraft carriers, were at sea and were saved.

The Pacific war

The Japanese immediately implemented their war plans and throughout the Pacific region they took one island after another, such as Wake Island and Guam. In the Philippines, where the American and Philippine forces were commanded by General Douglas MacArthur, the campaign opened with another US disaster as Japanese aircraft swept in undetected (despite prior knowledge by the US command in the islands of the attack on Pearl Harbor), destroying the majority of US aircraft on the ground at Clark Field. Japanese landings were not strongly opposed and MacArthur withdrew his forces to the Bataan peninsula. At this point President Roosevelt ordered a reluctant MacArthur to Australia to take command of all Allied forces in the South Pacific area, and he arrived on March 17 1942. Meanwhile, the Japanese increased their pressure on the remaining US troops moving down the Bataan peninsula, eventually taking the island fortress of Corregidor on May 6. Resistance from both US and Philippine forces had been much stiffer than the Japanese anticipated, as a result of which the campaign had lasted much longer than they had expected.

The Japanese advance in the Pacific continued at a decreasing rate, and in a significant and extremely hard fought action at Buna-Gona in Papua they were actually pushed back by a combined Australian-US force and forced to evacuate the island in January 1943.

Similarly, the Americans landed on Guadalcanal in the Solomon Islands in August 1942 and gradually overpowered the Japanese garrison until the remnants – some 13,000 men – escaped by sea in the first week of February 1943. Both the Papua and Guadalcanal campaigns, however, showed how stubbornly the Japanese fought in defence and were a warning of some very bloody battles to come.

In early May 1942 the first great carrier battle took place at the Battle of the Coral Sea, where an American task force commanded by Admiral Fletcher, who had been alerted by decrypted Japanese radio messages, met a Japanese force heading for Tulagi. The first engagement occurred on May 7 when US planes sank the Japanese carrier *Shohu* and a large number of Japanese fighter and bomber aircraft were shot down. On the following day the US carrier *Lexington* was sunk and *Yorktown* damaged, while the Japanese *Shokaku* was severely damaged. Both sides then withdrew.

This was, however, only the prelude to one of the decisive naval battles of history, which took place off Midway Island on June 4-6 1942. The Japanese planned a major fleet operation to enable an amphibious landing to be made on Midway, but once again the US Navy intercepted and decrypted the battle order, giving them full details of the plan including the timings. Thus, when the Japanese operation began with an attack on the Aleutian Islands, Admiral Nimitz was able to send a small force to deal with it, knowing that it was a diversion. Meanwhile he had gathered his

carriers together, including the damaged *Yorktown* whose repairs, estimated to take 90 days in peacetime, were completed in 48 hours.

The Japanese commander, Nagumo, closed on Midway confident that the majority of US forces were rushing off to defend the Aleutians and launched half of his aircraft at 0300 on June 4 1942, the other half remaining on board armed with armour-piercing bombs and torpedoes for possible anti-naval strikes. Meanwhile, US land-based aircraft from Midway Island were despatched, half to attack the Japanese carriers and half to attack the

ABOVE: The carrier USS *Lexington* (CV-2) explodes on May 8 1942. The Battle of the Coral Sea was the first of the great carrier battles and took place because an intercepted and decrypted Japanese message enabled US Admiral Fletcher's task force to be in the right place to intercept the Japanese invading the island of Tulagi.

BATTLE OF MIDWAY

Commanders	START STATES				LOSSES	
	Imperial Japanese Navy				US Navy	
	Carrier force (Nagumo)	Invasion force (Kondo)	Main fleet (Yamamoto)	Fletcher/ Spruance	Japanese	American
Men					3,500	307
Aircraft carriers	4	1	1	3	4	1
Battleships	2	2	7		–	–
Cruisers: heavy light	2 1	8 2	– 3	8 –	1 –	– –
Destroyers	11	21	21	15	–	1
Aircraft depot ships	–	2	–			
Tankers	–	6	–			
Transports	–	20	–			
Midget submarine carriers	–		2			
Aircraft: carrier-based land-based					275 –	}113 } 38

approaching bombers. Neither US effort was very successful mainly because, at this stage, Japanese aircraft were superior; the US aircraft heading for the carriers failed to score any hits, while the Japanese bombing raid managed to fight its way through to the island, where it caused a lot of damage.

Informed that a second attack on Midway was necessary, Nagumo ordered the weapons on the remaining aircraft to be changed to enable them to attack land targets. His men were part-way through this task when news was received that a major US naval force had been sighted to the northeast. The unfortunate flightdeck crews were ordered to cease what they were doing and reload the aircraft with naval strike weapons. The US carriers launched their aircraft, but their dive bombers missed the Japanese fleet in the murk and when their torpedo bombers launched their attack they not only failed to score any hits but 35 out of 41 were shot down. The Japanese were briefly confident of victory but five minutes later the US divebombers appeared and attacked the carriers, three of which were hit and sank later in the day, one being assisted by three torpedo hits from a US submarine. The fourth carrier, *Hiryu*, escaped undamaged and was able to launch two strikes against *Yorktown*, crippling it. By now, however, US aircraft had found *Hiryu*, which was hit and so severely damaged that it sank the following morning.

In the night four Japanese cruisers sortied against Midway but spotted a US submarine and, in trying to avoid it, two of the ships collided and the mission was cancelled. The two damaged cruisers limped homewards, surviving an attack by B-17 bombers, but were then attacked by carrier aircraft which sank one of them.

Thus, over a two day period the Japanese Navy had lost all four of its heavy carriers and Admiral Yamamoto, covering Nagumo from the north, tried to recover the situation by trapping the US ships into an engagement with his battleships. Admiral Spruance was not to be drawn and he pursued the withdrawing Japanese fleet until short-

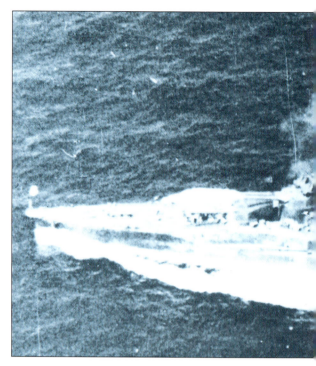

age of fuel forced him to turn home. Meanwhile, *Yorktown*, which had been limping towards Pearl Harbor escorted by a destroyer, was found by a Japanese submarine and both were torpedoed and sunk

It was an epic battle. The US lost one aircraft carrier, one destroyer, 132 land- and carrier-based aircraft, and 307 men. The Japanese, however, lost four carriers, one heavy cruiser, 275 aircraft and 3,500 men. The thousands of Americans involved in the combat fought with great skill and courage, but the reason they were in the right place at the right time in the first place was a handful of cryptanalysts in far-off Hawaii who had broken Japan's Fleet Code.

The war at sea was unremitting, since both sides knew that naval supremacy was the key, and there were many further remarkable episodes. The campaign off Guadalacanal lasted from early August to February 7, one of the longest ever, with two skilful opponents inflicting serious losses on each other, although in the end the Japanese withdrew the surviving 13,000 troops without loss, but the Americans triumphed as they held the island.

BELOW: US Marines storm Tarawa in the Gilbert Islands in November 1943. The fighting on all the Japanese-occupied islands was extremely bloody, with virtually every Japanese soldier fighting to the very end, forcing the attacking US troops to clear out every single position before they could consider the objective taken.

ABOVE: In the Battle of Cape Engano (October 25 1944) Japanese battle-ship *Ise* defends itself from attack by US dive-bombers, just before it was unsuccessfully attacked by submarine *Halibut* (SS-232). The large flightdeck aft was fitted in 1943 after the heavy loss of carriers in the Battle of Midway.

LEFT. A gun crew aboard the Australian destroyer HMAS *Arunta* bombard Japanese cargo ships during Operation Reckless, the invasion of Hollandia in May 1944.

The Americans, aided in MacArthur's command by the Australians and New Zealanders, were soon on the offensive, identifying the Japanese weak points and attacking them, soon exposing the myth of the invincible Japanese. Thus, the Allied forces on land could now take on the Japanese infantry in the jungle with confidence, while night fighting at sea was no longer an arcane art, and new tactics and machines enabled the air forces to shoot down the vaunted Japanese fighters such as the Zero in ever increasing numbers.

The Pacific islands were reconquered by the United States forces in increasing numbers. Makin, Tarawa, the Solomons, Hollandia, Kwajalein, Saipan and many others were taken, all at considerable cost as the Japanese soldiers and sailors defended every foot of territory. The US landing at Saipan, for example, was made on June 15 1944 and the island was not totally conquered until July 13, but in that time 27,000 Japanese were killed, 2,000 were captured, and many committed suicide, the military by traditional means using sword or pistol, while several hundred civilians jumped from cliffs. American losses, although grievous, were not on the same scale: 3,126 dead, 13,160 wounded and 326 missing.

By January 1945 US forces were back in the Philippines and on February 19 they landed on Iwo Jima and on April 1 on Okinawa. This last demonstrated the scale and sophistication attained by American amphibious tactics at this stage of the war. The landings were preceded by two weeks of operations by carrier groups and land-based aircraft to isolate the intended battlefield, attacking airfields, and intercepting air strikes, particularly by *kamikaze* aircraft.

ABOVE: One of the most famous pictures of World War Two as US Marines plant 'Old Glory' atop Mount Suribachi, Iwo Jima, February 23 1945.

Next, on March 23, aircraft and naval gunfire support started a relentless bombardment of Japanese positions on the islands, while troops secured two nearby islands for use as a fleet anchorage and support base. The action opened with a simulated landing to mislead the enemy while the main landing, involving some 60,000 troops, took place unopposed on April 1, with III Marine Corps on the left and the Army's XXIV Corps on the right. The marines encountered little opposition on the north of the island, but XXIV Corps, swung south and hit the enemy's main position, which was well sited, in great depth and held by very determined troops.

The Japanese responded with a series of *kamikaze* attacks. First came a strike against the US amphibious fleet by some 700 aircraft, half of them *kamikaze*, in which 383 attacking aircraft were downed, but two destroyers, two ammunition ships, one minesweeper and one landing ship were lost, and over 20 others damaged. The second phase of the attack consisted of a naval *kamikaze* group

consisting of a cruiser and eight destroyers, headed by the giant battleship *Yamato*, which was spotted by US submarines. US carrier aircraft found *Yamato* just after midday and carried out one attack after another until at 4.23 pm the blazing hulk sank, taking 2,488 sailors with it. Further aircraft *kamikaze* attacks were targetted on the ships on supporting the landing on April 12 and 13, claiming more ships, but at the end there were no Japanese aircraft or pilots remaining, while there were still vast reserves of US ships, equipment and manpower.

The battle on Okinawa continued until a stalemate was reached where the US forces were stopped by the main Japanese opposition, while the Japanese were unable to dislodge the Americans. The Japanese were finally overwhelmed on June 22, having lost 107,500 dead, plus another 20,000 (estimated) who were sealed in caves, with just 7,400 becoming prisoners-of-war, whereas the Americans lost some 12,400 dead and 36,000 wounded.

The Far Eastern war – Burma and India

The Japanese attacked the British colony of Hong Kong on December 8 1941, taking the New Territories on the mainland on December 10 and the island itself on December 25. The Japanese had established forces in French Indochina some months previously (as a result of German pressure on Vichy France) and this was used as the springboard for the invasion of Malaya, with the first troops landing on December 8. The Japanese then drove southwards, outmanoeuvreing the British at almost every turn and reaching the southern tip of the peninsula on January 31. A brief pause preceded crossing to the island of Singapore, where, following a sharp but short fight, the British garrison surrendered on February 15 1942.

The naval war also got off to an inauspicious start. On December 10, the British battleship *Prince of Wales* and battlecruiser *Repulse*, having tried and failed to find the invasion fleet, were detected by Japanese torpedo bombers based at Saigon and, lacking any air defences, were sunk in a one hour attack – a devastating blow both to British naval prestige and to the naval balance of power between the Allies and Japan.

While this had been going on in the Pacific, the Imperial Japanese Navy had been extending Japan's reach in the West. Allied forces composed of American, British and Dutch ships attempted to oppose the Japanese invasion of the Dutch East Indies, but suffered heavy losses. The Dutch territory surrendered

on March 9 and the Japanese seized the Andaman Islands in the Indian Ocean on March 23; whereupon the Japanese First Air Fleet (which had carried out the attack on Pearl Harbor) sortied into the Indian Ocean between March 25 and April 8, sinking one British carrier, two cruisers and a destroyer without any loss to themselves. The British fleet withdrew to Dar-es-Salaam and commanders became so concerned that the Japanese might attempt to seize the island of Madagascar (which was under Vichy French control) and thus dominate most of the Indian Ocean, that they invaded the island on May 5, handing the island over to de Gaulle's Free French on January 8 1943.

Burma

The Japanese invaded Burma from Thailand on January 12 and at first carried all before them. They pushed back the small British forces, took Rangoon on March 7 and then advanced up country towards India, outflanking British defences one after another. The Chinese sent two divisions to help, commanded by US 'Vinegar Joe' Stilwell, but by June the

Japanese were in control of virtually the whole of Burma, while the British were hastily constructing defensive positions at Imphal and preparing for a Japanese invasion of India.

In December 1942 the British began a carefully orchestrated, small-scale advance in the Arakan, the prime objective being to restore morale by inflicting a defeat on the overextended Japanese. The Japanese reacted strongly and by May 12 the positions were exactly as they had been in December. In a separate effort, again intended to show that the Japanese were not 'supermen', British Brigadier Wingate formed a special operations brigade, known as the 'Chindits', to operate deep behind Japanese lines. His 3,000 strong force set out in mid-February and succeeded in cutting one of the two railways that had been their objectives, but they were forced to withdraw, harried by the Japanese, and straggled back to the British line in April having lost about one-third of their number.

A further British drive in the Arakan was more successful than the first and by April 1944 had advanced some distance, but was then held up by the monsoon, resulting in a

ABOVE: A British anti-aircraft battery during a Japanese raid on the island of Hong Kong during the brief siege in December 1941. The scene is almost surreal, with the immaculately dressed troops, the pristine gun positions, the gun controllers in front of the gun muzzles and the spotter's arm-chair on the right.

BELOW: A Japanese *kamikaze* sweeps in on his final attack on the carrier USS *White Plains* (CVE-66) off Leyte on October 25 1944. He was unsuccessful, crashing into the sea close to the carrier's stern.

ABOVE: The Chindit operations were intended to prove to the British that they were as good at jungle warfare as the Japanese. In this they succeeded, but the cost was high, with many casualties, like this Gurkha soldier, although casualty evacuation by light aircraft was a very welcome innovation.

stalemate lasting from May to December 1944. The second Chindit expedition, five brigades strong, set out on March 5, and again operated behind Japanese lines. The originator of the force, now Major-General Wingate, was killed in an air crash and, although the operation was more successful than the first, it still resulted in heavy casualties for little overall gain.

Meanwhile, the Japanese launched the long-awaited invasion of India, crossing the Chindwin River on March 6 1944, but, to the Japanese surprise, two British garrisons held out. The small garrison at Kohima was isolated on April 5 but survived in bitter fighting until a relief force arrived on April 20. The larger garrison at Imphal was also involved in heavy fighting, not least because the Japanese plan depended upon capturing the British supplies. The British in Imphal were, however, reinforced and resupplied by air, standing firm until the Japanese Fifteenth Army was forced to withdraw as a result of high casualties and sickness, coupled with shortage of supplies, ammunition and food.

In 1945 the British, under General Slim, went on to the offensive, sweeping southwards through Burma, and now it was their turn to outmanoeuvre and outfight the Japanese. They crossed the Irrawaddy river on January 14, captured Mandalay on March 21 and reached Rangoon on May 2. They were preparing to mount an invasion of Malaya when the war ended in August.

The submarine war

The Japanese submarine service was composed of carefully selected men in the largest submarines and with the best torpedoes of any belligerent nation. The service scored a few isolated successes, but overall it did not acquit itself well, for reasons which have never been adequately explained. One feature of their campaign, however, was a series of atrocities against survivors, unparalleled in any other submarine service.

On the other side, the US Navy submarine service had a magnificent record. Over 250 submarines saw service in the Pacific, of which

LEFT: A USAAF B-25 Mitchell takes off from USS *Hornet* (CVA-8) on April 18 1942. This exceptionally courageous operation, led by Lieutenant Colonel Doolittle, was the first air raid on the Japan homeland. The last was on August 9 1945, when the second A-bomb was dropped on Nagasaki.

185 had sunk at least one enemy ship, and some of them many more than that, with the total coming to some 200 warships and over 1,000 merchant ships. Some 52 US submarines were lost, 37 of them with all hands. US submarines were used for a wide variety of purposes, including anti-shipping, radar picket and rescue for fliers on long-distance raids.

The air war

The Japanese started the war with strong air forces divided between the navy and the army, which carried out the attack on Pearl Harbor and made regular raids on targets such as Singapore and Rangoon until they surrendered. By far the most imaginative use of air power in the early part of the war, however, came from the United States when 16 USAAF B-25s, commanded by Lieutenant-Colonel Doolittle took off from the carrier *Hornet*, flew 800 miles (1,300km) to mainland Japan, bombed a number of cities including Tokyo, and then flew on to China or, in one case, to Russia. All 16 planes were lost; 71 of the crewmen survived, one died, and eight were captured, four of these being executed by the Japanese. The main effect of the raid was psychological, but it remains a splendid achievement.

BELOW: One of the early seaborne raids was undertaken by USS *Argonaut* (SS-168) which carried a party of US Marines to raid the Japanese base on Makin Island on August 18 1942. Here, *Argonaut*, then the largest submarine in the US Navy, awaits the return of the raiders.

OPPOSITE: Hiroshima in the vicinity of 'ground zero'. The world's first atomic bomb with a yield of 12.5 kilotons was exploded at a height of 1,670ft (510m), which counted as a 'surface burst'.

BACKGROUND PIC: Before the days of the *kamikaze*, a Japanese 'Val' dives on USS *Hornet* (CV-8) on October 26 1942.

BELOW: B-29s dropping conventional bombs on Japan. The atomic bombs gained greater publicity, but the conventional bombs wrought far greater destruction.

One of the major determinants in the US island-hopping campaign was the need for airfields for the strategic bombers, but these also flew from India and China. The first B-29s arrived in India in April 1944 and carried out their first raid against mainland Japan on June 15 1944, having staged through five new airfields in China. By the end of 1944 B-29s were operating on a daily basis out of the Mariana Islands and striking the Japanese mainland.

In July 1945 the United States found itself facing the prospect of an invasion of the Japanese homeland. Plans were made for such an operation which would have included a landing on Kyushu in November 1945 followed by a second on Honshu in March 1946. Although its fleet and air force had been destroyed, Japan still had some four million soldiers and if they had defended their wartime gains with grim determination, their defence of the homeland would have been even stronger Allied losses, particularly for the US, would have been extremely high.

Having considered all the factors, US President Truman decided that the atomic bomb should be used. The first was dropped on Hiroshima on August 6, when some 78,000 were killed, 70,000 wounded, and many others developed long-term radiation illnesses. A lack of reaction by the Japanese government led to a second bomb being dropped on Nagasaki on August 9, when some 40,000 were killed and 25,000 injured. Despite the power of these

attacks, which, of course, were each the result of a single bomb, the most destructive air raid of the war actually took place on March 9 1945 when 334 B-29 bombers dropped 1,667 tons of incendiary bombs on Tokyo. That raid created a firestorm similar to those at Hamburg and Dresden, and resulted in 83,000 people being killed and 100,000 injured.

Faced by these awe-inspiring bombing raids (and the Soviet entry into the war against Japan), the Japanese accepted the Allied surrender terms. The cease-fire was implemented on August 15 and the surrender took place on September 2. The Second World War was over.

WORLD WAR TWO ESTIMATED LOSSES – THE ALLIES

Country	Total forces	Military dead	Military wounded
China	8,000,000	500,000	1,700,000
France	6,000,000	211,000	400,000
Soviet Union	25,000,000	7,500,000	14,000,000
UK	6,000,000	400,000	475,000
USA	15,000,000	290,000	570,000
Other Allies	4,000,000	250,000	not known
TOTALS	**64,000,000**	**8,901,000**	**17,145,000**

WORLD WAR TWO ESTIMATED LOSSES – AXIS POWERS

Country	Total forces	Military dead	Military wounded
Germany	12,500,000	2,850,000	7,250,000
Italy	4,500,000	77,500	120,000
Japan	7,400,000	1,506,000	500,000
Other Axis	1,000,000	200,000	not known
TOTALS	**25,400,000**	**4,633,500**	**7,870,000 (+?)**

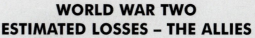

ABOVE: USAF Boeing
B-29 Superfortresses
drop bombs on a target
in North Korea. General
MacArthur was
dismissed by President
Truman for wanting to
use such aircraft
(possibly with atomic
bombs) against China.

Korean War 1950-1953

Korea was annexed by Japan in 1905 and on
several occasions during the Second World War
the Allies promised it full independence once
the war was over. The sudden end of the war in
1945 took the Allies by surprise and it was
hastily arranged that Soviet troops would
accept the Japanese surrender in the north and
US troops that in the south, the dividing line
being arbitrarily drawn at the 38th Parallel.
The United Nations promised countrywide
elections for a new government but the Soviets

disagreed and two separate states were
declared in 1948: the Republic of Korea (RoK)
in the south and the Democratic People's
Republic of Korea in the north.

On June 25 1950 the North Korean Army
(NKA) attacked in massive strength and without any warning, attempting to overrun the
south before outsiders could react. They
achieved considerable success and US forces
were rushed from Japan to stem the tide,
although by August 5 the RoK and US forces
were hemmed into a small pocket in the south-
east around the port of Pusan. Defence of the

RIGHT: A US Army
artillery battery fires
multiple rocket
launchers at enemy
positions during the
Korean War.

south quickly became a United Nations responsibility, with the legendary General Douglas MacArthur in command, and US forces were soon being augmented: first to arrive were aircraft of the Australian air force in August, followed by a British infantry brigade, despatched from nearby Hong Kong, in September.

On September 15 the US Army's X Corps landed at Inchon in one of the great outflanking moves of history. The North Koreans were totally taken by surprise and when the UN forces in the south broke out of the Pusan perimeter the NKA disintegrated and streamed northwards. When the UN forces were nearing the Chinese border, however, the People's Liberation Army (PLA) entered the fight and drove the UN forces back down the peninsula again, the 38th Parallel being reached by December 15. UN operations were not helped by the death in an automobile accident of the land forces commander, General Walker, who was replaced by Lieutenant-General Ridgeway, although MacArthur remained in overall command.

Having consolidated briefly on the 38th Parallel the PLA went on the offensive again on January 1 1951, pushing the UN back some 50 miles (80km), past the southern capital, Seoul. The UN forces were, however, far stronger and better organised than earlier in the war and having halted the PLA's advance they counterattacked, pushing steadily northwards. Seoul was retaken on March 14 and the general line of the 38th Parallel was reached by the end of March. At this point differences between MacArthur and President Truman came to a head and the president exercised civil supremacy by dismissing the general.

The PLA attacked on April 22 and pushed the UN forces back but then a UN offensive starting on May 22 reached a position a little to the north of the 38th Parallel where the US Joint Chiefs of Staff (JCS) ordered the commander to halt.

There then began a long series of 'on again-off again' negotiations which stretched from July 1951, with some limited UN offensive operations between August and November. These were not helped by the behaviour of South Korean President Syngman Rhee but the armistice was eventually signed on July 27 1953.

Suez War 1956

The events in the Middle East in 1956 must be seen against the background of the establishment of the state of Israel on May 14 1948 and the subsequent Arab-Israeli War, which was ended by a series of armistices, the last of which was signed in July 1949. A group of colonels overthrew the monarchy of Egypt in 1952, with Colonel Nasser emerging as the leader in 1955. He negotiated the withdrawal of the British garrison, which had occupied the Canal Zone for many years; the last men left in June 1956. Meanwhile, Nasser devised a plan to dam the Nile at Aswan, and when both the USA and the British withdrew promises to help finance the dam in July 1956, Nasser threatened to nationalise the Suez Canal, in order that he could use the revenues to finance construction of the dam.

SUEZ WAR 1956

	TOTALS INVOLVED		KILLED / LOSSES	
	British	French	British	French
Manpower:				
– land forces[1]	}	}	17	10
– naval forces	}45,000	}45,000	4	0
– air forces	}	}	1	2
Aircraft	300	200	8	2
Ships	100	30	0	0
[1] Including marines				

BELOW: British 'paras dropping on Gamil airfield at Port Said in the opening move of the very short-lived Anglo-French Suez campaign, November 5 1956.

RIGHT: The Anglo-French air forces carried out a major bombing programme from bases in Cyprus. Here a pall of smoke rises over a blazing oil farm in Port Said, with ships of the invasion fleet lying offshore.

The British and French decided to take joint action to retake the Canal, and coordinated their plan clandestinely with Israel. Unfortunately, shortage of equipment and lack of plans meant that the operation took a long time to organise and instead of attacking in late July, when the operation might have gained both national and international acceptance, nothing happened until October. Then, in accordance with the secret plan, Israeli paratroops dropped at the east end of the Mitla Pass on October 29 1956 while other units attacked overland. The Egyptians immediately despatched troops over the Canal and at 1800 on October 30 a combined Anglo-French ultimatum was issued to both sides, calling on them to disengage, withdraw and allow an Anglo-French force to occupy the canal to allow 'free navigation'.

The Anglo-French forces comprised some 90,000 troops, split roughly 50:50 between the two countries, some 500 aircraft (60% British) and 130 ships (75% British). Action started on October 31 with air attacks on Egyptian airfields and President Nasser ordered his troops to begin to withdraw from the Sinai in order to defend the Canal. Egyptian troops held El Agheila against repeated Israeli attacks, although a sudden advance southwards succeeded in taking Sharm-el-Sheikh on November 5, the sixth day of the war.

Meanwhile, desperate efforts at the United Nations eventually achieved a ceasefire, although not before the Anglo-French paratroops carried out an assault landing in the early morning of November 5, followed by an amphibious landing the following day. The Anglo-French troops pushed forward as hard as they could but the United Nations ceasefire came into effect at 1930 that evening and it was all over. After several days a United Nations force arrived, and the invaders returned to their ships and departed.

The whole operation was a fiasco, showing up the basic weaknesses of both Britain and France. While neither was forced out of the Middle East as a direct result, their prestige and influence in the area have never recovered. The time taken to organise the Anglo-French command structure and the obvious lack of preparedness, particularly among the British forces, did nothing to enhance the success of the operation. The irony is that had they struck quickly the chances of success, particularly in the international sphere, would have been good.

BELOW: One of President Nasser's counter-moves to the invasion was to sink a large number of ships in the Suez Canal, which closed the waterway for many months.

Vietnam War 1965-1973

Background

The sudden collapse of the French position in Indochina (see page 63) following their defeat at Dien Bien Phu led to the 1954 Geneva Accords. These provided for:

• a ceasefire
• Cambodia and Laos to become independent states
• Annam, Cochinchina and Tongkin to be split into two independent states, divided at the 17th parallel by a demilitarized zone (DMZ)
• nationwide elections on the possibility of reunification to be held by the end of 1957.

As a result, the Democratic Republic of Vietnam (DRVN) was established in the north, with its capital in Hanoi; it was ruled by the Viet Minh, becoming a de facto Communist state (North Vietnam). The second new state, the Republic of Vietnam (RVN), was established in the south with its capital in Saigon.

US STRENGTHS AND LOSSES IN VIETNAM

	US military strength	US deaths
1965	15,400	
1966	389,000	4,771
1967	480,000	9,699
1968	536,040	14,437
1969	484,326	6,727
1970	335,794	7,171
1971	158,119	942
1972	24,200	531

BELOW: Described by many Westerners as 'little men in black pyjamas', Viet Minh soldiers such as these defeated first the French, then the Americans and, finally, the South Vietnamese.

US IN VIETNAM 1965-73

		Maximum strength[1]	CASUALTIES					
			Died in combat	Wounded	Prisoners/ missing	Non-battle deaths	**TOTALS**	
USA	Army	440,691	30,644	76,811	2,904	7,173	**117,532**	[1] March 1969 figures.
	Navy	37,011	1,477	4,178	788	880	**7,323**	
	Marines	86,727	12,953	51,389	144	1,631	**66,117**	[2] Estimated figures.
	Air Force	61,137	1,152	933	1,650	592	**4,327**	
	TOTALS	625,566	46,226	133,311	5,486	10,276	**195,299**	[3] Australia Republic of Korea (RoK)
South Vietnam		1,000,000[2]	196,863	502,383	not known	not known	not known	New Zealand Philippines Thailand
Other free world[3]		72,000	5,225	11,988	not known	not known	not known	
North Vietnam/ Viet Cong		1,000,000[2]	900,000[2]	1,500,000[2]	not known	not known	not known	

One of the earliest problems was that South Vietnam was an entity for which nobody (not even the French) had made any preparations and a prominent and respected Vietnamese, Ngo Dinh Diem, was summoned to become prime minister. In October 1955 Diem deposed the titular head of state (the former Emperor Bao Dai) and proclaimed a republic with himself as president. Diem's regime rapidly became corrupt, while the Communist insurrection continued, the new enemy being dubbed the 'Viet Cong'. The US government poured in ever-increasing amounts of military aid, which was administered in-country by a body set up in 1956 with the designation Military Assistance Advisory Group (MAAG), upgraded to Military Assistance Command in 1962.

Meanwhile top elements in the South Vietnamese military and civilian structure devoted as much effort to internecine power struggles in Saigon as to the fight against the Viet Cong in the countryside. Diem became increasingly autocratic and, after several failed coup attempts, success was achieved in November 1963 when both Diem and his brother were assassinated and a general took over.

On August 2 1964 several North Vietnamese fast attack craft were alleged to have attacked a US destroyer in the Gulf of Tongkin, and US Navy aircraft immediately carried out retaliatory strikes against DRVN naval bases. This led to the US Congress passing the 'Gulf of Tongkin Resolution' which gave the president wide-ranging powers in South-East Asia and US involvement in the war rapidly increased. The original commitment had been to provide supply bases, but then helicopter units had deployed to support the Army of the Republic of Vietnam (ARVN), followed later by USAF aircraft to give direct tactical support. The US had also taken over from the French the task of providing military advisers to the ARVN. For some time the major threat was considered to be a conventional invasion by the DRVN so the US trained the ARVN in conventional war techniques. The real threat, however, came from the Viet Cong conducting guerrilla warfare and in early 1965 the Viet Cong targeted US bases in South Vietnam, which led to the US carrying out retaliatory air strikes against the North. On February 7 1965 US installations at Pleiku were attacked, which was considered to be a hostile act against the USA and on March 8 1965 the President invoked the Gulf of Tongkin resolution and marines of the 9th Marine Expeditionary Brigade landed on the coast near Danang, followed by the Army's 173rd Airborne Brigade in May. It had now become an American war and was run by the US commander in South Vietnam, Lieutenant-General William C. Westmoreland.

The US at war

Once it had been decided to commit US troops the build-up was rapid, with total strengths reaching 50,000 in June and 181,000 in December. The first B-52 bomber strike took place on June 18 while the first major US ground operation was launched on June 28.

BELOW: North Vietnamese infantry, with the nearest man armed with a Chinese Type 69 40mm anti-tank grenade launcher (copy of Soviet RPG-7).

LEFT: As over Germany, Japan and Korea, USAF strategic bombers were also used over North Vietnam.

Deploying throughout the country, US units immediately undertook aggressive action against the NVA and the Viet Cong, leaving the ARVN to conduct the campaign in the rural areas. This was the era of massive firepower, 'search-and-destroy' missions, and body counts. Not surprisingly, the US forces won virtually every engagement they became involved in, although the strain of the war both domestically within the United States and on the international scene began to be intolerable.

On January 30 1968 some 50,000 NVA and Viet Cong suddenly unleashed the Tet offensive, attacking some 30 urban targets throughout South Vietnam, with the principal attacks in Saigon and Hué. In fierce fighting the attackers sustained some 30,000 casualties, with the Viet Cong being particularly hard hit, but they failed to crack the ARVN and the

anticipated mass uprising failed to occur. For the North it was an undoubted military defeat and it was a disaster for the Viet Cong, although in a war full of contradictions the attack turned out to be a major psychological success on the international scene giving the impression, strongly reinforced by the media, that the United States could never win the war. As a direct result of the Tet offensive, President Johnson announced that he would not stand for re-election, the preliminary negotiations ('talks about talks') were opened with the DRVN and a bombing halt was ordered.

While this was going on, a major battle was taking place at Khe Sanh just below the Demilitarised Zone (DMZ) where a force of 6,000 US Marines was surrounded by 20,000 NVA troops in a situation somewhat similar to that at Dien Bien Phu. The base had originally

BELOW: 6,000 US Marines dug in at Khe Sanh and invited the North Vietnamese Army to do its worst. Unlike the French at Dien Bien Phu, the Marines were given adequate air and artillery support and they held out until the NVA had had enough.

been used by Special Forces to train Montagnards and was later used by the Marines to prevent the NVA using a short cut from the DMZ to the Ho Chi Minh Trail. The outcome was, however, different from Dien Bien Phu as the Marines had massive air power on call and they were able to resist the enemy attacks until a relief force arrived. The Marines put up a strong resistance, but it also appears possible that the NVA did not really want to overrun the garrison as they had at Dien Bien Phu; the capture of 6,000 US Marines would have given them a serious administrative problem and could also have united popular feeling in the USA in the face of a massive military humiliation.

Nixon was elected US president in November 1968 and formal negotiations with the DRVN started in January 1969, with the first token US troop withdrawals taking place in July. Throughout this, operations continued, with an NVA offensive in February/March and a major military success for the US at the Battle of Hamburger Hill in May.

The bitter fighting continued throughout South Vietnam in 1970. US forces and the ARVN conducted a joint operation in February/March near the Cambodian border where they found vast NVA logistic stocks and destroyed them. This was followed by a countrywide NVA/VC attack on over 100 US and ARVN facilities, but although the fighting was fierce it lasted less than a week, because logistic difficulties forced the attackers to curtail the operation and withdraw. Then on April 30 a second US/ARVN operation against NVA/VC supply depots commenced, involving some 40,000 US and ARVN troops, but this time the US troops crossed into Cambodia in pursuit of their aim; the operation ended on June 30.

In 1971, the first major event was an ARVN incursion into Cambodia and Laos in February. Huge amounts of military hardware were seized including 106 tanks, large numbers of trucks and many weapons. Meanwhile, the peace negotiations continued and the US drawdown proceeded apace, with responsibility for all ground operations being transferred to the ARVN on August 11, although US air operations continued.

A visit by top DRVN politicians to Moscow in 1972 secured Soviet agreement to a major invasion of the South, which began on March 30 1972 and was known as the 'Easter invasion'. Because the VC had never recovered from the 1968 Tet offensive, the 'Easter invasion' was essentially an NVA affair, using conventional tactics on three fronts. One thrust was in the north in the area of the DMZ; the second was in the centre, aimed at cutting South Vietnam in two; and the third was in the south, in and around the Mekong Delta. The invasion

last US combat troops left Vietnam on March 29. Meanwhile the NVA increased its overall strength to some 20 divisions, and continued to resupply and reinforce its units in the south, while on the other side the ARVN was forced to reduce, in part because of increasingly severe reductions in US aid.

By the start of 1975 South Vietnam was on the brink of disaster. The NVA had a free run along all the borders and controlled substantial areas within in the South. With the benefit of hindsight, the correct military course would

achieved some successes, with the capital of the northern province, Quang Tri, falling on May 1, but it soon ground to a halt, partly as a result of logistic problems, but also because many determined ARVN divisions fought the NVA to a standstill and much lost ground was eventually regained. Quang Tri, for example, was retaken on September 15 after very heavy fighting. President Nixon ordered the mining of DRVN harbours and interdiction of land and sea routes, and the North Vietnamese returned to the conference table. The NVA had repeated the same error as against the French in 1951 by going on to the offensive and conducting large-scale operations before they were ready for it. Consequently, logistics problems abounded, with tanks running out of fuel, and infantry/tank cooperation was poor. So, the NVA withdrew from the battlefield and, as always, they learnt their lessons and waited to fight another day.

The formal ceasefire agreement was announced on January 23 1973 and became effective on January 28, but February 12 was even more significant in the United States as the first US prisoners of war were released. The

have been for the ARVN to withdraw its forces from the northern part of the country to concentrate on the defence of the heartland around Saigon, but it would have been politically impossible to abandon millions of people. As a result the ARVN continued to be spread thinly over the entire country and when the enemy attacked it was unable to hold anywhere.

The final phase, when it came, was mercifully brief. In a preliminary move, the NVA overran Phuoc Binh province in the first week of January and then unleashed its full offensive in the Highlands in March. Finally, South Vietnam President Thieu ordered the elite airborne division to redeploy from the north to Saigon, but this led inevitably to panic among the civil population and by March 18 the ARVN had started to collapse in the north and west. By now the NVA was on the general offensive, capturing Hué on March 25 and Danang on April 1. The end was now clearly in sight and, while some individuals managed to reach the US naval forces waiting offshore, the collapse accelerated and Saigon fell on April 30. The long war – it had lasted no less than 30 years – was over.

ABOVE: Soldiers of a long-range patrol team of Company D, 151st (Ranger) Regiment engage the Viet Cong. The nearest man holds a 5.56mm M16 rifle, a weapon whose reputation was established in the Vietnam War.

RIGHT: A shot-down US airman, barefoot and bandaged, is escorted through a Hanoi park to a press conference, where he will be urged to denounce his 'imperialist' political leaders.

BELOW: The 8 inch (203mm) guns of USS *St Paul* (CA-73) firing against a target in South Vietnam.

The air war

The US and ARVN forces were given massive air support. Direct tactical support was provided by the US 7th Air Force, which had nine bases in South Vietnam and another two in Thailand, while giant B-52 bombers came in from Guam and other bases to carry out both strategic strikes in the North and tactical sup-port to US and ARVN in the south. In addition, there were US Navy and US Marine Corps aircraft operating from both land bases and aircraft carriers, and a large force of US Army aircraft. On top of that were the aircraft of the South Vietnamese Air Force, and aircraft from the various 'Free World' contingents.

Against this massive force the DRVN could field only small numbers of MiG-17, -19 and -21 fighters, SAMs and anti-aircraft guns. Despite the lack of sophistication compared with the US aircraft, these defences inflicted very heavy casualties, USAF losses alone between January 1962 and August 1973 being 2,257 aircraft and 2,118 men killed.

One of the most devastating and flexible weapons in the war was the Boeing B-52 Stratofortress bomber. These remarkable air-craft flew 124,532 missions over a period of eight years and two months, in the course of which they dropped 2,674,745 tonnes (2,949,000 short tons) of ordnance. No fewer than 18 aircraft were brought down by enemy action (15 of them during Linebacker II), while another 13 were lost in mid-air collisions and other accidents.

The war included one of the most devastat-ing exhibitions of the use of airpower when President Nixon unleashed Operation Line-backer II as a reprisal for the North Vietnamese having abandoned the Paris peace-talks on December 13 1972. The initial opera-tion lasted for three days, starting on the night of December 18. Out of a planned 129 B-52s, 121 attacked in three waves, supported by F-111s which attacked four MiG bases, and F-4 Phantoms which sowed chaff corridors. The North Vietnamese fired over 200 SAMs and much AA ammunition and also flew many MiG sorties, bringing down three B-52s and damaging two others.

Day 2 was more successful for the USAF and no aircraft were lost but on Day 3 six aircraft were lost. The aircrew were critical of the tactics and after a reappraisal the instructions were changed. These and other steps reduced the losses on Days 4 to 7 and there was then a 36-hour 'Christmas truce' before 113 B-52s in seven waves struck targets in and around Hanoi, Haiphong and Thai Nguyen over a 15 minute period. The defences were overwhelmed and only two B-52s were shot down. The operation continued for another three days and then the DRVN signified its willingness to return to the negotiating table.

Linebacker II lasted 11 days during which 729 missions were flown from U-Tapao in Thailand (340) and Guam (389), during which 15 aircraft were lost and nine damaged, all to SAMs. Over 49,000 bombs were dropped (13,605 tonnes) on 34 discrete targets. The effect on the ground was devastating and caused the DRVN major problems, particularly on communications systems, although they claimed that only 1,300-1,600 civilians were killed.

The sea war

Throughout the war, the US Navy had absolute command of the sea. The incident which sparked off direct US involvement occurred in the Gulf of Tongkin. The retaliatory strikes were mounted from carriers standing off the coast of the DRVN and the first combat troops ashore – Battalion Landing Team 3/9 – came from embarked marines. Thereafter the Navy was continuously engaged,

with four-five carriers on 'Yankee station' off North Vietnam and one carrier on 'Dixie Station' off Cam Ranh Bay, while the northern region was a Marine Corps area throughout the war.

Other Navy activities included a coastal blockade of the coast of South Vietnam to prevent smuggling of warlike equipment for the north, riverine patrols and shore bombardment, including from the Iowa-class battleships.

The lessons

The war showed that even a military superpower was prevented from waging all-out combat in a situation short of general war. Thus, the US forces in Vietnam were constantly subjected to limits imposed by the Pentagon in response to directives from the White House.

Media attention became a very significant adverse factor for US forces, but never for the NVA and Viet Cong. Television meant that events taking place in Vietnam were screened within hours in the United States, bringing enormous emotional pressures to bear on families and politicians. Further, every event and every new strategy was dissected and discussed endlessly in the media, something which the US armed forces found very difficult to come to terms with. Popular sentiment in the USA became a very significant factor in the war and many of those who did not belong to the vociferous minority which actively opposed the war considered it to be a mistake.

BELOW: A North Vietnamese Army missile crew run to bring their SA-2 Goa surface-to-air missile system into action. Despite a lack of sophistication the NVA defences shot down no fewer than 2,257 US aircraft in the course of the war.

ABOVE: Two of the British Challenger II tanks, part of the Coalition Army which inflicted a devastating defeat on Saddam Hussein's army in the Gulf.

Second Gulf War 1990-1991

Background

In April 1990 Iraq's leader, Saddam Hussein, pressurised the tiny sheikhdom of Kuwait over financial matters, including writing off $US5 billion loans made during the Iraq/Iran war and an increase in OPEC oil prices. He also demanded the transfer to Iraq of two small islands and of certain oilfields in the north of Kuwait, together with a payment of $US2 billion for oil he considered 'stolen' from those wells. Kuwait rejected all the claims and Saddam's threats were generally regarded as hot air. Thus, reports on July 31 that Iraqi troops were massing near the border with Kuwait were regarded as crude attempts to influence the Kuwaiti delegation at talks. At the next meeting the Kuwaitis walked out and on August 2 1990 Iraqi troops poured over the border and took just 48 hours to establish full control, with an announcement on August 9 that Kuwait had been annexed as Iraq's 19th province. The crisis rapidly grew worse, with captured Westerners being used as hostages. International response was surprisingly firm and rapid, with Western and Arab nations forming a Coalition of forces to oppose Iraq. The first foreign troops, a brigade of the US 82nd Airborne Division, arrived in Saudi Arabia on August 9.

There was constant activity at the UN. A blockade was imposed on August 25, followed by an air embargo on September 25. This culminated in an ultimatum to Iraq on November 18, which stipulated that Iraqi forces would be expelled from Kuwait by force if they had not vacated the sheikhdom by January 15 1991.

Warlike operations started on January 16 with a series of Coalition air strikes which continued until February 22. Aircraft struck military and infrastructure targets such as transportation hubs and communications centres, using a mixture of guided and 'smart' munitions, as well as iron bombs. Up to February 21 both sides incurred aircraft losses, the Coalition 21 and Iraq 40. In a surprise move, some 140 Iraqi aircraft flew to Iran, where they were interned; the crews were later repatriated but, as far as is known, the aircraft remain on Iranian airfields to this day. This phase also saw the first operational use of US land-, sea- and air-launched cruise-missiles, which were able to attack specific targets with pinpoint accuracy, taking out high-value targets in a way that had never previously been possible.

Another feature of this phase was the use by Iraq of Scud surface-to-surface missiles. These had been used by Iran against Iraq with limited success during the first Gulf War, but on this second occasion they had a dramatic effect. There were approximately 80 launches of which 50 per cent were aimed at Israel, a country not even involved in the conflict. There was particular anxiety that the Iraqis would use chemical warheads, which they were known to possess and had used against both Iranian and Kurdish targets. In the event there is no evidence that they ever did so.

The ground war

The first ground operation preceded the war proper and was a somewhat half-hearted Iraqi operation, in which a force of approximately brigade strength attacked the deserted Saudi Arabian towns of Wahfrah and Khafji just before first light on January 29. A rapid response by Coalition forces comprising Saudi and Qatari troops and US Marines retook Wafrah on January 30 and Khafji on January 31. Once this action was over ground operations appeared to stagnate, although there was, in fact, a lot going on.

The ground war was one of the great military triumphs of the modern era. Coalition operations began at 0400 (local) on February 23 and it quickly became obvious that a major reshuffle of formations had been going on, unseen by the Iraqis and unreported by the media. The assault consisted of three major elements:

1. On the left was XVIII (US) Corps, consisting (from left to right) of 6th (French) Light Division, 82nd (US) Airborne Division, 101st (US) Airborne Division, 24 (US) Infantry Division (Mechanized) and 3rd (US) Armored Cavalry Regiment. Apart from the French, this was the US Army's Rapid Deployment Force (RDF), which had not only trained together but had actually prepared for several years for a possible campaign in Saudi Arabia.

2. In the centre was VII (US) Corps, consisting of 1st (US) Armored Division, 2nd (US) Armored Cavalry Regiment, 3rd (US) Armored Division, 1st (UK) Armored Division, 1st (US) Infantry (Mechanized) Division, and 1st (US) Cavalry Division.

3. On the right were:
- Joint Forces Command (North) composed of two division equivalents of Egyptian, Syrian and other Arab forces.
- Marine Central Command, comprising 2nd (US) Marine Division; Tiger (US Army) Brigade; and 1st (US) Marine Division.
- Joint Forces Command East, which moved along the coast.

BELOW: A Kuwaiti oil jetty ablaze: part of the vengeful gestures inflicted by the Iraqi forces when they realised that defeat was inevitable.

The speed of the advance was astonishing and a large number of pre-war concerns proved to have been without foundation. The berms (sandhills) were insignificant obstacles, the vaunted Iraqi artillery contributed almost nothing to the defence, and the Iraqi Republican Guard (a so-called 'elite' force) was only marginally better than the confused, ill-equipped and ineffective troops that made up the bulk of the Iraqi Army.

The objective was the recapture of Kuwait but the forces on the left had the task of sweeping round to the River Euphrates with the aim of both cutting off reinforcements and preventing a withdrawal into Iraq by the forces in Kuwait. The 6th (French) Light Division was on the left, protecting XVIII Corps' open flank and the Corps swept forward with great verve, far exceeding its planned rate of progress. In the centre VII (US) Corps contained virtually all the Coalition forces' heavy armor and it swept all before it.

SECOND GULF WAR COALITION TROOP CONTRIBUTIONS

Country[1]	Troops	Tanks	Attack helicopters
Argentina	100		
Bangladesh	6,000		
Great Britain	35,000	177	18
Canada	400		
Egypt	35,000	450	
France	17,000	40	70
Gulf States	17,000	200	
Honduras	200		
Morocco	1,500		
Niger	500		
Pakistan	5,500		
Senegal	500		
Saudi Arabia	45,000	200	
Syria	20,000		
Turkey[2]	100,000		
USA[3]	2,050	1,158	380
TOTALS	**285,250**	**2,225**	**468**

[1] The following countries contributed non-combat medical teams: Australia, Hungary, New Zealand, Poland, Sierra Leone, Singapore, Sweden.
[2] These were positioned in Turkey on the Turko-Iraqi border.
[3] Excludes assets afloat.

REGIONAL CONFLICTS AND MAJOR CIVIL WARS

Boer War 1899-1902

The years 1900 to 1914 saw the final phase of European colonial expansion and were marked by numerous minor conflicts in Africa and Asia. Such conflicts had very localised effects, but there were three more important regional conflicts which contributed significantly to the build-up of international tension, and led, albeit indirectly, to the First World War: these were the Boer War; the Italo-Turkish War; and the Balkan Wars.

The turn of the century found the British at war with the Boers (the descendants of the original Dutch settlers at the Cape of Good Hope in Africa) in a conflict which had been continuing since 1880, in which territorial and cultural disputes between Afrikaaners and Anglo-Saxons were considerably exacerbated by the discovery of gold, diamonds and other precious minerals. The Boer War proper began in October 1899 with the Boers laying siege to Mafeking and Kimberley, and the British quickly found themselves launched into a totally new type of war.

Since the Crimean War, they had become used to small engagements against poorly organised and badly equipped Asian and African enemies, but now they found themselves fighting men of European stock, who were well-armed, extremely well trained as marksmen, and who used guerrilla tactics. As usual in British wars, the original generals did badly and were sacked, and the new commander, General Roberts, first reorganised the British forces and made them more mobile, before advancing. He defeated Boer General Cronje at Paardeburg on February 27 1900 and relieved Ladysmith the following day, although the Boer's siege of Mafeking was not raised until May 18. The war then became a guerrilla campaign in which the highly mobile Boers raided at will, while the British tried various tactics to bring them under control. In the final phase Boer farms were burnt, while large numbers of Boer women and children were forced into camps to stop them providing sustenance to their menfolk. The name of these assembly points – concentration camps – introduced a new term to the politico-military vocabulary. The war ended in May 1902, with surprisingly generous terms going some way to easing the bitterness engendered in the final phase of the conflict.

BELOW: Boers were well-armed, lightly equipped, knew the country well – and ran circles around the British until the latter became more mobile and adjusted their tactics to the needs of the wide-open veldt.

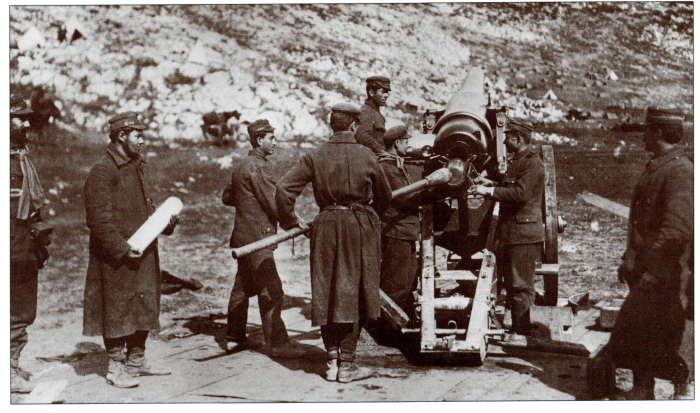

Italo-Turkish War 1912

In the Mediterranean, Italy had observed the French expanding along the North African littoral with some alarm and decided to grab the only remaining territory – Libya – for itself. Libya was then part of the Ottoman Empire and the Italo-Turkish War began with Italian naval bombardments of Libyan ports on September 29 1911, following which troops were put ashore. These enclaves were later expanded, but in April 1912 the Italian Fleet threatened to attack the Dardanelles, and then invaded Rhodes and some smaller Turkish-ruled islands in the Dodecanese. The Treaty of Ouchy in October 1912 resulted in Italy gaining Libya, Rhodes and the Dodecanese Islands.

The Balkan Wars 1912-1913

The war with Italy had exposed the Ottoman Empire's military weakness, and Bulgaria, Greece and Serbia formed the Balkan League to attack the remaining Turkish European provinces in Albania, Epirus and Macedonia in October 1912. Known as the First Balkan War, this consisted of a confused series of battles in which the League generally bested the Turks, following which the major European powers tried to bring peace to the area in a conference held in London. The conference started in December 1912 and collapsed within a month, but intense diplomatic efforts led to it being reconvened in May 1913, and the Ottoman Empire was deprived of virtually all its remaining European possessions. The Balkan League

countries then fell out among themselves in a dispute over the fruits of the recently concluded war and Bulgaria attacked the other two in May 1913. Romania also joined in against Bulgaria, while Turkey seized the opportunity to reoccupy Adrianople. This Second Balkan War ended in July 1913 with Bulgaria having lost everything it had gained from the first war while Turkey regained a few of its losses. The confused politics, frequent regrouping and general bad faith left a legacy of mistrust of 'Balkan affairs' which not only led to the First World War but has lasted in Europe to the present day.

TOP: In the Balkan wars, a Greek gunner is about to ram an old breech-loading gun while another soldier waits with the charge.

ABOVE: In the Second Balkan War Albanian gunners await developments in the old fortifications overlooking the harbours at Durazzo.

Mexican Revolutions and US-Mexico War 1916

Mexico suffered a series of revolutions throughout the 19th Century and was also invaded by French forces in 1861. It was ruled by a firm dictatorship under Diaz from 1877 until he was overthrown in 1911, but then no leader was able to establish undisputed control for some years. Pancho Villa, one of several contenders for power, attacked the US town of Columbus, New Mexico on March 9 1916 and killed 24 Americans before being driven off with heavy losses. The US president immedi-

from January to November 1919. The conflict was temporarily halted when the Allies imposed an eastern border on Poland, but this failed to satisfy the Poles who attacked on April 25 1920, starting the Russo-Polish War. Commanded by General Pilsudski, the Polish forces captured Kiev and then tried to outflank the main Russian army commanded by Marshal Tukhachevski, but instead the Russians outmanoeuvred the Poles and forced them to withdraw. Pilsudski sensed that the Russians had over-extended themselves and, in a dramatic counter-attack, struck at their centre, while Sikorski came in from the north,

ABOVE: A group of Mexican rebels man a well-built trench during one of the many revolutions.

ately deployed a large military force to the border and a punitive expedition, led by Brigadier-General Pershing, was sent into Mexico with the aim of capturing Villa, in which it failed. The force was withdrawn in March 1917, in time to form the nucleus of the US military forces sent to France for the First World War.

trapping the Russians between two Polish pincers. The Russian forces were routed, although Tukhachevski managed to rally his troops briefly before being pushed back even further by the victorious Poles. The war ended with an armistice on October 12 1920 in which Poland achieved all its territorial claims.

Russo-Polish War 1920

Poland has had a more troubled history than almost any other European country and was dismembered by the Congress of Vienna in 1815 which shared it out between Austria, Prussia and Russia. None of these masters was popular and the idea of Polish nationhood never died, leading to periodic insurrections. On November 11 1918 (the day the Armistice was signed) Poland became effectively independent and Pilsudski took power. There were several border conflicts, including one with Ukraine and another with the newly-created Czechoslovakia, but the most serious was with Soviet Russia, the first phase of which lasted

Greco-Turkish War 1920-1922

The victorious Allies occupied Constantinople (now Istanbul) following the end of the First World War, although conditions elsewhere in Turkey approached anarchy. In May 1919 the Allies authorised the Greeks and Italians to send troops to protect their nationals and thus a Greek army went to Smyrna (in ships supplied by the Allies) while Italian units landed in South-West Anatolia.

Meanwhile, Turkish General Mustafa Kemal established a Nationalist government at Ankara and when, following a successful Greek offensive, the Allies attempted to impose a treaty on the Sultan, it was rejected by

Kemal's Nationalist movement. The situation was further complicated in October by the death of the Greek king, who was succeeded by his father, Constantine, a man so mistrusted by the Allies (because of his behaviour during the First World War) that they removed their support for Greek operations in Turkey.

The Greeks achieved some small military successes in early 1921, but then King Constantine took personal command of his army, winning a major victory at Eskisehir in July. Mustafa Kemal then took personal command of the Turkish army and conducted a campaign which rapidly gained momentum, eventually forcing the Greek army back into Smyrna, from where it was evacuated in early September 1922. Mustafa Kemal then marched on Constantinople where he negotiated an end to the war and abolished the Sultanate. The situation was finally resolved in July 1923 by the Treaty of Lausanne, whereupon the Allied force departed and Kemal, now renamed Atatürk ('Leader of the Turks'), set about modernising his country.

Chaco War 1932-1935

The inter-war years were generally peaceful in South America, the exception being the Chaco War between Paraguay and Bolivia. Clashes began in 1928 leading to open warfare in 1932 in which Bolivia initially did well, not least because it employed a German general to command and train its forces. Paraguay then retrained its forces, expanded its army, gained control of most of the Chaco region and cap-

tured some 30,000 prisoners. A truce was signed in 1935, but the treaty ending the war was not completed until 1938, when Paraguay achieved most of its war aims.

Ethiopian-Italian War 1935-1936

The Ethiopian-Italian War began with a series of clashes on the border between Ethiopia and Italian-occupied Somaliland, which Italy used as a pretext to invade Ethiopia in October 1935. Condemned by the League of Nations, this led to a League of Nations trade embargo against Italy, which proved to be totally ineffective. The Ethiopians were totally unable to oppose Italian air power and had no defence against the poison gas which was used against them. Not surprisingly, Italy gained control, annexing Ethiopia to the newly-created Italian Empire in May 1936.

ABOVE: Abyssinian infantry in the Ogaden region scramble back on to the road to continue their advance after Italian warplanes have passed.

BELOW: Abyssinian troops under training in May 1935. When the Italians invaded, the Abyssinians fought bravely but were no match for modern technology, and the world was unable to prevent the Italians from bombing and using gas against these ill-prepared troops.

RIGHT: Chinese troops resist the Japanese advance in Shanghai in February 1932.

BELOW: Japanese with drawn swords clearing a building in Nanking. They are all carrying gas respirators on their backs; as the Chinese did not possess gas weapons, this was presumably a precaution against its use by their own side.

Sino-Japanese War 1937-1945

Japan expanded wherever possible in East Asia from the middle of the 19th Century. During the First World War it joined the Allies and after the war it was given all the former German possessions in Asia north of the Equator, including the German Pacific islands, together with Tsingtao and a number of smaller conces-sions in mainland China. In the 1920s Japan provided most of the troops for the interna-tional force which protected the International Settlement at Shanghai.

The Chinese Civil War in the 1920s (see page 82) provided Japan with an excellent opportunity to expand the areas under its con-trol and clashes with the Nationalists gave the pretext to take over Shantung province between May 1928 and May 1929. Tension increased rapidly in 1931 when, in response to the Japanese takeover of Manchuria, the Chinese people boycotted Japanese goods and the Japanese landed an army in Shanghai which eventually defeated the Chinese defend-ers. In February 1932 Manchuria was made a Japanese protectorate with former Emperor Pu Yi on the throne, following which in early 1933 the province of Jehol was annexed on the grounds that it 'belonged' to Manchuria. Japanese pressure on China culminated in the 'China incident' on July 7 1937 when a clash with Chinese troops, deliberately engineered by the Japanese, gave the latter the excuse to invade and start the Sino-Japanese War.

The Japanese armed forces were large, well-equipped and well-trained, with large reserves of manpower and great industrial capacity at home in Japan, against which China had a large, but poorly trained army, with only a minimal navy and air force, and very limited and backward defence industry. To add to China's problems it had suffered from a debilitating period of unrest during the 'war-lord' period, followed by the first phase of the Nationalist/Communist civil war. Throughout the war with Japan, China was defended by two groups – the Nationalists (Chiang Kai Shek) and the Communists (Mao Tse-tung) – which spent part of the time actually fighting each other and even when they fought the Japanese they tended to do so within the context of how it would affect the eventual outcome of the civil war.

Not surprisingly, the Japanese gained much territory, although their brutal methods ensured that they never gained the support of the civil population, and they also suffered some military setbacks (for example, at

Taierchwang and Chengchow, both in 1938). The war in China ended suddenly when the atomic bombs forced Japan to surrender to the Allies in August 1945.

First Indochina War 1945-1954

Background
The original European presence in Indochina came from French and Spanish missionaries and in the 1850s local rulers sought to limit their activities. Feelings ran high and the murder of a Spanish bishop led to a Franco-Spanish naval force being despatched, which captured and held Saigon in what was then Cochin China. The French rapidly increased the area under their control, gradually taking control of all five states, which were grouped together into the colony of French Indochina.

Foreign rule was never totally accepted and

LEFT: A Japanese single-engined bomber over China during the mid-1930s. Such tactics ensured that the Japanese never obtained any support from the civil population.

FRENCH INDOCHINA TERRITORIES

	Capital	Population	French protect-orate	Remarks
Empire of Annam	Hué	6,000,000	1884	Prior to French arrival, Annam extended from the Chinese border to Saigon.
Kingdom of Cambodia	Phnom - Penh	3,100,000	1863	
Cochin China	Saigon	4,600,000	1868	Originally part of Annam, but ceded to France in 1868.
Tongkin	Hanoi	8,000,000	1883	
Kingdom of Laos	Vientiane	1,000,000	1893	

ABOVE: Logistic support is a major problem in any war and more so for a revolutionary army. The Viet Minh solved it with these bicycles, which, with simple adaptations (note the sticks in the handlebar and on the saddle column) could be used to move food, ammunition, radio batteries - in fact, almost anything the army needed.

there was continuous unrest, which periodically took the form of riots, and which was eventually focused in the Communist movement, founded by Ho Chi Minh in the mid-1920s. During most of the Second World War the French colonial authorities were legally under the direction of the Vichy government in Metropolitan France, which meant that they had to cooperate with the Japanese. Allied help in resisting the Japanese occupation was, therefore, directed towards the Communists.

The Vietnamese People's Liberation Army (VPLA) was created in 1941, with the first regular unit being raised in 1944, while the civil side of the movement created a parallel administrative structure; the whole organisation was known collectively as the Viet Minh. On the sudden Japanese surrender in 1945 the Allies divided the country into two at the 16th Parallel, with Chinese Nationalist troops

responsible for the north and British troops for the south. These troops arrived in Hanoi (September 16) and Saigon (September 13) respectively to find that the Viet Minh had already taken control, although relationships were at first reasonably amicable. The Viet Minh were actively opposed to a return to French rule, but the French did return, encouraged by the British in the south, and they later also negotiated a return to the north.

War against the French

Despite some early cooperation, relations between the Viet Minh and the French quickly deteriorated and by the end of 1946 the Viet Minh had taken to the hills and were conducting a guerrilla campaign against the French colonial power. The Viet Minh were following a doctrine (developed from the teachings of Mao Tse-tung) of a three stage campaign in which:

Stage I. The revolutionary movement was on the strategic defensive, using guerrilla tactics to stretch out the government forces, while concurrently building up its own infrastructure.
Stage II. Strategic balance is maintained during which guerrilla tactics are used to keep the government stretched, while regular (main force) units are raised and trained.
Stage III. The revolutionary movement goes on to the offensive, attacking and defeating government main force units and gradually taking over control of the country.

Foreign powers quickly became involved as supporters of the two sides. The Soviet Union provided diplomatic and financial help and equipment to the Viet Minh, while the USA provided similar help to the French as part of their overall strategy of containing what appeared to be a series of Soviet-inspired guerrilla campaigns throughout the Third World. A major change in the situation occurred in 1949 when the Communists in China overcame the Nationalists and arrived on the Tonkin-Chinese border. The Chinese then not only provided military aid, but were also able to provide an 'active sanctuary' in which the Viet Minh could train and rest, secure from French attack.

Stalemate

By 1950 the French position was so acute that the country's most illustrious soldier, Marshal de Lattre de Tassigny, was sent to take over as both commander-in-chief and as high commissioner, giving him absolute military and political control of the war. A charismatic leader, de Lattre led from the front and on several occasions when important positions were threatened he flew in and took personal command. During one such incident his chief of staff sent a plaintive signal from Saigon sug-

FRENCH FORCES AT THE BATTLE OF DIEN BIEN PHU

ORIGIN	On completion of fly-in	At start of siege				Reinforcements by air			
	Dec 6 1953[1]	March 13 1954[2]				March 13 to May 6 1954[3]			
	TOTAL	Officers	NCOs	Enlisted	TOTAL	Officers	NCOs	Enlisted	TOTAL
Metropolitan France		180	477	755	1,412	92	303	1,003	1,398
Foreign Legion		97	309	2,563	2,969	31	131	800	962
North Africa[4]		2	167	2,438	2,607	–	1	29	30
Other Africans[5]		–	8	239	247	–	–	–	–
Vietnamese[6]		1	202	3,376	3,579	10	68	1,823	1,901
TOTALS	**4,907**	**280**	**1,163**	**9,371**	**10,814**	**133**	**503**	**3,655**	**4,291[7]**

[1] No breakdown of this figure is available.
[2] The day of the start of the battle
[3] All parachuted in, except for 14 who were air-landed.
[4] From French territories, including Algeria, Morocco and Tunisia.
[5] From French territories, including Senegal, Niger, etc.
[6] These were a mixture of regulars and auxiliaries.
[7] 680 of these were NOT qualified paratroops; all were making their first operational jump; some were making their first-ever parachute jump; all were volunteers.

gesting that he should not be there, to which de Lattre sent the classic reply: 'Come and get me.' Unfortunately for France, de Lattre became ill from cancer and had to be relieved in 1952.

De Lattre was succeeded by General Salan, a paratroop officer, who also actively prosecuted the war, although by now the Viet Minh had moved on to their third stage and were deploying divisions. The Viet Minh had also developed a remarkable logistic system, based on the use of porters pushing heavily loaded bicycles through the jungle and over mountains; it was a slow and manpower-intensive system, but it worked.

Battle of Dien Bien Phu

The battle of Dien Bien Phu (November 20 1953 to May 7 1954) was an historic turning point, not only in the war in Vietnam, but also globally, since it demonstrated that a guerrilla army could turn itself into a conventional army and defeat a Western army in a set-piece battle. General Navarre (who had taken over from Salan) planned to attract the Viet Minh main force into a battle on ground of his own choosing and selected Dien Bien Phu, a small village in North-East Tongkin, some 190 miles (300km) outside the area held by French troops. The French operation started on November 20 when paratroops dropped on

BELOW: Operation Camargue in 1953 and a Vietnamese unit under French command moves away from the beach after the landing. The vehicle on the sky-line is a US-supplied tracked landing craft.

the village, began to construct a defensive position and restored the existing airstrip so that normal infantry units could fly in to relieve the elite paratroop units, who were needed elsewhere. Assisted by engineers, the new arrivals built a main stronghold of seven strongpoints in the north, each named after a woman: Anne-Marie, Beatrice, Claudette, Dominique, Elaine, Francoise and Gabrielle. There was a further subsidiary position some 5 miles (9km) to the south, designated Isabelle. The fortress was commanded by Colonel de Castries and included ten M24 tanks, which were broken down into their components, flown into the garrison in freighter aircraft and then reassembled.

Taking up the challenge, General Giap moved his main force towards Dien Bien Phu, although he originally used only two divisions to invest the stronghold, sending the other two on a raid into northern Laos. Navarre made a number of miscalculations: placing the defensive position on the floor of a valley surrounded by hills; assessing that the Viet Minh could not bring artillery through the jungle; and deciding that the Viet Minh would not be able to interfere with the air support of the garrison in the valley.

It was a battle in which artillery played a vital role. When the battle proper started in March, the French artillery commander mustered four 155mm and 24 105mm howitzers, and 32 120mm mortars, all of which were flown in. In addition, some 95,000 rounds of 105mm ammunition and 8,500 rounds of 155mm had to be parachuted in once the siege started. Against this, thousands of Viet Minh

porters dragged in 144 75mm and 105mm howitzers, 48 120mm mortars, 30 75mm recoilless guns, 36 37mm anti-aircraft guns and 12 6-barrelled Katyusha rockets. These weapons were pulled through the jungle, across rivers and up hills to get them into position and, once there, gun positions were dug *inside* the hilltops so that they could bombard the French with relative impunity. Nor was it only the guns that had to be pulled, but every round of ammunition had to be carried with some 150,000 being fired between March 13 and the end of the battle.

Navarre intended to seize the initiative, but it was Giap who decided when, where and how he would attack, the date he chose being March 13. The Viet Minh artillery opened with a massive barrage from the hills and their infantry started to take French positions immediately. Beatrice fell just after midnight on March 13/14, followed by Gabrielle on March 15, at which point the French artillery commander, appreciating the enormity of his blunders, committed suicide. Anne-Marie fell on March 18. On April 1, Giap felt strong enough to attempt an all-out attack, but after heavy losses he was compelled to withdraw in order to counteract what were termed 'rightist tendencies' (ie, low morale) among the Viet Minh ranks.

By May 1 Giap was ready to try again and this time there was no mistake. The French garrison was forced slowly inwards until, on the evening of May 7, the Viet Minh overwhelmed the remnants. The siege had lasted 56 days, during which the Viet Minh lost 8,000 dead and 15,000 wounded. The French, on the

BELOW: Cheerful and confident, French paras land at Dien Bien Phu on November 20 1953. At first sight it was a strategic master-stroke, but the French built their strongholds in the valley while the Viet Minh took over the hills looming in the background. It was a costly error which led to defeat, first at Dien Bien Phu and then in Indo-china as a whole.

other hand, lost over 2,000 dead, 7,000 wounded (virtually all of whom became prisoners) and 7,000 prisoners; just 73 men managed to escape into the hills.

It was, by any standard, a great military victory, in which an Asian army, raised from nothing just ten years previously had out-generalled and outfought a major European army. The political consequences were equally important, because news of the fall of Dien Bien Phu reached Europe on the day the Geneva Conference on the future of Indochina started, placing the French in an impossible position. Above all, it gave the Viet Minh the confidence that would sustain them throughout another war, this time against an even more powerful, much better equipped and even more determined enemy.

ABOVE: A French soldier carries a dead comrade from the aid post at Dien Bien Phu.

BELOW: Victorious Viet Minh troops hoist their flag over the ruins of General de Castries' command post.

Arab-Israeli Wars 1948-present

Background

A state of hostility has existed between Israel and its Arab neighbours since the foundation of the State of Israel on May 14 1948. This long period has been characterised by virtually non-stop terrorism interspersed with periodic escalations into outright conflict. All these conflicts have been complicated – and made far more dangerous – by the involvement of outside powers, whose aid to one or more participants varied from diplomatic support, through covert military support and weapons supply, to outright involvement.

First Arab-Israeli War (1948-49)

The First Arab-Israeli war broke out the day the state of Israel was established by the UN. On the Arab side were regular units of the armies and air forces of Egypt, Iraq, Lebanon, Syria and Transjordan, supported by a large number of Palestinian Arabs, all of which varied in standards of training, efficiency and morale. Against them were the forces of the newly created state, comprising some 30,000 troops, supported by settlement guards and former terrorist groups. Equipment varied, but high morale was bolstered by the knowledge that this was a battle for survival.

Fighting was bitter from the start, with some early Arab successes, but it halted with a UN-brokered truce between June 11 and July 9 1948. The second phase lasted from July 9-18 and was followed by yet another truce, while the UN mediator, the Swedish Count Bernadotte, endeavoured to find a solution. Bernadotte was murdered on September 17

and the truce began to break down as the Jewish forces gained in both confidence and numbers. Fighting restarted in October as the Israelis consolidated their gains and ceasefires in the north enabled them to concentrate their

RIGHT: An extraordinary sight as two antiquated Dragon Rapide biplane light transports fly top cover for an Israeli ground convoy taking supplies to besieged communities in the 1948 Arab-Israeli war.

efforts in the south to drive the Egyptians back. The new UN mediator, Dr Bunche, then chaired armistice negotiations in Rhodes between Israel and each of its opponents, the last of which was signed in July 1949.

Second Arab-Israeli War (1956)

The chain of events leading to the Suez War started with the US withdrawal of its promise to help finance the planned Aswan Dam, following which Nasser nationalised the Anglo-French-run Suez Canal, which gave rise to a secret plan for cooperation between France, Israel and the UK. The Anglo-French attack on the Canal is described elsewhere (see page 47). The Israelis started the war (as agreed with the British and French) with a parachute battalion landing on the Mitla Pass on October 29 1956, while the remainder of the brigade joined it on the second day, having fought its way across the desert. There were several days of intense fighting, in which the Israelis were by no means always successful, before the Egyptians began to withdraw towards the Canal. Fighting continued up to November 5 when the Anglo-French forces landed at Suez and the conflict was brought to an end on November 6.

ABOVE: The Israelis found wrecked Spitfires and parts abandoned by the withdrawing British and quickly restored them to operational status. A further 60 Spitfires were purchased from Czechoslovakia.

BELOW: An Israeli B-17 bombs Cairo in 1948.

ABOVE: Triumphant Egyptian soldiers place their national flag atop the Israeli Bar-Lev Line which was captured on October 13 1973 in a brilliant operation.

ABOVE RIGHT: An Israeli gun crew fires its US-supplied 175mm gun against Syrian positions on the distant Mount Hermon in a routine exchange of fire.

Third Arab-Israeli War (Six-Day War) (1967)

The 1967 Six-Day War followed a month of deteriorating relations between the various Arab countries and Israel, and, calculating that war was inevitable, Israel attacked first on June 5, carrying out a series of devastating air strikes on Egypt in the morning, Jordan and Syria in the afternoon, and Iraq in the evening. On the southern front Israeli forces struck hard against the Egyptians who, on the second day, started to withdraw behind the Suez Canal. Despite sporadic outbreaks of hard fighting, the Israelis were on the banks of the Suez Canal by June 8 and a UN ceasefire was agreed on the following day. On the other fronts, the Israelis took Jerusalem on June 7 and the Golan Heights on June 9, the final ceasefire coming into effect on June 10. One of the significant incidents in this war was an Israeli air attack on USS *Liberty*, an electronic surveillance ship, which was standing some 14 miles (22km) off the coast, near El Arish.

The October (Yom Kippur) War (1973)

The next war took its name from the Jewish feast of 'Atonement' (Yom Kippur). It started on October 6 1973 with a brilliant Egyptian success. Egyptian forces took the Israelis com-

pletely by surprise, when an air strike was followed by an assault crossing of the Suez Canal, and within hours bridges had been built and tanks were across. The Egyptians then consolidated but were forced to advance in order to take pressure off their Syrian allies. Thereafter things went wrong for the Egyptians, as the Israelis attacked along the inter-army boundary and were soon across the Suez Canal. Two Israeli divisions were eventually on the Egyptian side of the canal but a ceasefire came into effect before they could force the Egyptian 3rd Army, trapped in the Sinai, to surrender. In the north the Syrians also achieved initial success and came close to recapturing the Golan Heights before they, too, were pushed back. This campaign was notable for the successes achieved by Soviet-made missiles: SA-N-6 and Strela against aircraft and RPG-7 and 'Sagger' against tanks.

The USA and USSR became dangerously involved in this war, with both organising air lifts at short notice to resupply their clients in the Middle East. Matters escalated when the USSR placed seven airborne divisions on short notice to move, to which Washington responded by raising the alert status of US forces worldwide. Once again, however, the UN brokered a ceasefire between the Arabs and Israel.

Arab-Israeli confrontation (1973-96)

In the years following the October War there has been constant conflict in and around Israel centring on two issues: Israel's search for a secure existence and the Palestinians' demand for their own homeland. The conflict has taken a variety of forms, ranging from isolated incidents to major military operations, but has, so far at least, fallen just short of war.

Terrorist incidents have included the hijacking of an airliner to Entebbe (June /July 1976), the massacre of Israeli civilians on the coastal road (1978), the *intifada* (uprising of Palestinians against Israeli occupation forces) and a whole series of bombing incidents. Most Israeli responses have been on a 'tit-for-tat' basis, usually involving shelling or bombing the terrorist positions in Lebanon. The Israeli army has moved into Lebanon on several occasions, including the Litani River attack (March 1978) and the invasion of Lebanon (June 1982). There have also been some long distance operations, including the rescue of the hostages in Entebbe, Uganda (July 1976); the air attack on the Iraqi nuclear reactor (June 1981); and the air attack on the PLO headquarters in Tunis (October 1985).

Invasion of Lebanon (1982)

In 1982 the Israelis responded to increasing PLO attacks from bases in Lebanon by invading the country on June 6 1982. On the ground three divisions drove deep into Lebanon: one on the right up the Beka'a Valley, the second in the centre and the third along the coast, the latter being supported by amphibious landings by commandoes. The Israelis made steady progress on land, while the air force took out virtually all the Syrian-operated SAM sites, and from then on enjoyed total air supremacy. Although the Israelis took on the Syrians if they met them, they made it clear that their primary target was the PLO.

By the sixth day the Israelis were investing Beirut and they sought to force the PLO and Syrians to leave the city. Diplomatic negotia-

BELOW: Israeli soldiers relax after taking part in the capture of Jerusalem on June 8 1967.

ABOVE: Israeli warplanes bombed this Beirut street just minutes before a cease-fire was due to go into effect, and Lebanese start searching for survivors and for bodies.

tions eventually resulted in a plan which was accepted by all sides, and the PLO left Beirut, mostly by sea. Unlike previous Israeli military undertakings, the invasion of Lebanon was heavily criticised domestically and was also widely condemned internationally. Criticism increased when it became known that some 400 Palestinian civilians had been massacred by local militiamen in two refugee camps; although the militiamen were subsequently found to be responsible, Israeli commanders and troops were alleged to have been aware of the danger of such events and to have failed to prevent them.

In 1983 the Israelis withdrew southwards and a multinational force deployed into Beirut, composed of French, Italian, UK and US troops. These units suffered two devastating suicide attacks, in which 58 French troops and 241 US Marines were killed. The force remained until March 1984, when all withdrew, having achieved little, but at considerable cost. The fighting in Lebanon has continued for many years.

First Gulf War 1980-1988

Background

One of the major disputes between Iran and Iraq concerns the Shatt-el-Arab, the river running north-westwards from the Persian Gulf which separates the two countries. A 1937 treaty gave most of the river to Iraq, although Iran had always claimed that the mid-point was the true demarcation line. There was a cri-

sis in 1969 when Iran abrogated the treaty, but despite warlike demonstrations from both sides hostilities were confined to sporadic border clashes, although the quarrel rumbled on, pursued by the Khomeini regime as much as it had been by the Shah.

War breaks out

The situation escalated in September 1980 when Iraq suddenly invaded, capturing the town of Khoramshah and penetrating some 30 miles (50km) into Iran. There then ensued a long period of stalemate when the two sides made repeated attempts to break through the opposition's front-line but with little success; loss of life was, however, heavy on both sides. In March 1982 the Iranians felt sufficiently confident to initiate a campaign intended to push Iraqi forces out of their country. The first phase lasted from March 22-30 1982 and met with some success, driving the invaders back some 25 miles (40km), and was followed by a second in May/June which resulted in the recapture of Khoramshah, taking the Iraqi garrison with all its weapons.

The Iraqis proposed a truce and implement-

LEFT: Iraqi troops fire a Soviet-supplied field gun during the war against Iran.

ed a unilateral ceasefire, but Iran responded by adding the removal of President Saddam Hussein to their war aims. The Iranians started a new offensive in mid-July, which included air raids on Baghdad, and yet another offensive followed later in the year.

In February 1983 the Iranians sought to reach the Basra-Baghdad road, one of Iraq's strategic highways, but after some initial progress they were halted and then pushed back by an Iraqi counter-attack. Throughout the remainder of 1983 there were repeated attacks by both sides, all of which failed in their objectives and by now oil installations had become targets for both sides. One Iraqi offensive in February 1984 included the use of mustard gas.

The war ground on through 1986 when the Iranians captured the Faw peninsula. This was followed by a change of direction by the Iraqis who adopted a more offensive strategy and expanded their army. 1988 saw the 'War of the Cities' when Iraq employed its Soviet-supplied Scud missiles in attacks on Iranian cities. Considerable damage was caused and the attacks had considerable psychological effect.

Western involvement

One of the effects of this protracted war was to draw the West's attention once again to the vulnerability of its oil supplies, and Western warships were regularly deployed to the Gulf to seek to exercise some form of protection over oil facilities and the tankers. Unfortunately, this also meant that these ships occasionally became involved in the war. One major incident took place on May 17 1987 when the frigate USS *Stark* was the target of an Iraqi attack, using an air-launched Exocet missile; 37 men were killed and considerable – but repairable – damage was inflicted. Iraq claimed that the attack was a mistake and apologised.

In a second incident, the US cruiser *Vincennes* was carrying out the first operational deployment of the Aegis command-and-control system when it detected an Iranian aircraft climbing out of Bandar Abbas. Due to a series of errors the command post crew believed that the aircraft, actually an airliner, was diving towards the ship and, since it failed to reply to the ship's electronic interrogator, a missile was fired and the aircraft was shot down with the loss of 290 civilian lives.

BACKGROUND PIC: The Iraqis have often set fire to other peoples' oil terminals; this pall of smoke rises over an Iranian pipeline at Abadan in 1980.

ABOVE: An Indian Army T-62 main battle tank advances during the brief war with Pakistan in 1971. India crushed the forces in East Pakistan, which then broke away from the distant West to become the autonomous state of Bangladesh.

Final stages

The war dragged on, with both sides apparently content to maintain hostilities at a level they could sustain for years. Iraq moved on to the offensive in 1988 and carried out some successful attacks but without breaking the strategic stalemate. On August 20 a UN-brokered ceasefire was signed by both sides and the war came to an end, leaving Iraq internationally isolated and very deep in debt, which was to prove a recipe for disaster (see page 56).

India-China War 1962

A long-running dispute over borders in northeast India erupted into war in October 1962, when Chinese forces attacked on two separate fronts, some 1,000 miles (1,600km) apart. The Chinese were very successful and, having achieved their aim, declared a ceasefire and withdrew to the outer limits of the disputed territory, making it difficult for India to continue the war. This defeat caused India to reform and modernise its armed forces.

India-Pakistan War 1965

Another border dispute, this time with West Pakistan, led to India's next conflict. The border dispute was in the Rann of Kutch, a barren region, and erupted into some 14 days of fighting in April-May 1965. Operations ceased with the onset of the monsoon and attention swung to Kashmir, where border clashes started in August, leading to the invasion of Kashmir by Pakistan on September 1 1965. The situation was complicated by a Chinese threat to attack Indian troops in the Himalayas. Diplomatic efforts by the UK, UN and USA brought hostilities to a halt by the

end of September, although the tension between India and Pakistan continued at a high level.

India-Pakistan War 1971

When it was created in 1947 to accommodate the Indian sub-continent's Muslim population, the state of Pakistan consisted of two wings: West Pakistan and East Pakistan. Although the people of both 'wings' were Muslims, those of West Pakistan were, in general, the better educated and more sophisticated, predominating in the upper ranks of the armed forces and the civil service. Civil disturbances broke out in East Pakistan in March 1971 which were suppressed by the Pakistan Army with considerable severity. India provided sanctuary for

escaping East Pakistanis and initiated a policy of tempting Pakistan into taking the first step in a major war. Pakistan fell into the trap and conducted a series of air raids on Indian air bases on December 3 1971.

The Indians were fully prepared and escaped the worst effects of the air strikes. The Pakistani attack, however, gave India the excuse it needed to undertake a massive land attack on East Pakistan, to which Pakistan responded by attacking Kashmir. As so often in modern conflicts there were energetic moves in the distant UN to bring about a ceasefire but the Soviets vetoed the resolution, since their allies, the Indians, were on the verge of success. The Pakistani Army in Dacca surrendered on December 16 and a ceasefire was agreed the next day. Bangladesh obtained its independence, which it retains to this day.

Indonesian 'Confrontation' 1963-1966

Indonesia, a former Dutch colony, achieved independence in 1949, but for many years thereafter there was a series of minor 'post-colonial' conflicts. The first was in West Irian (West New Guinea) which had been retained by the Dutch, but after several years of low-key military activity the Dutch agreed to withdraw. Attention then turned to the island of Borneo, of which Indonesia owned the largest (southern) share, but with the British territories of North Borneo and Sarawak, and the indepen-

dent Sultanate of Brunei along the northern coast.

In December 1962 Indonesia backed an attempted coup in Brunei, which was quickly put down by the British. The formation of the Federation of Malaysia in September 1963 was, however, strongly opposed by the Indonesian leader Soekarno, who initiated a form of undeclared war, which he described as 'Konfrontasi' (= confrontation).

The conflict was, in the main, confined to low-level jungle warfare on the island of Borneo, although several Indonesian military groups landed on the mainland of West Malaysia, in an effort to foment a 'popular uprising', but were very rapidly rounded up. All was not well within Indonesia, however, and a pro-Communist coup was brutally suppressed by the army, culminating in a military coup in March 1966. This was followed by a conference in Bangkok, Thailand, and a ceasefire was agreed in June.

ABOVE: Indonesian guerrilla soldiers train villagers in ambush drills during the war against the Dutch colonial power in 1949.

LEFT: Irregulars of the Mukti Bahini threaten a column of handcuffed collaborators after the surrender of the Pakistan Army in December 1971. The crowd looks cheerful enough, but in such situations can turn vicious within a few seconds.

Soviet War in Afghanistan 1979-1988

Russia shares a long border with Afghanistan and has interfered in the smaller country's affairs since the middle of the 19th Century. This meddling increased during the Cold War and Soviet influence was behind the coup that deposed the king in 1973. The new government sought to impose rapid change on the country, causing great resentment among a staunchly Muslim population, especially in the countryside. Armed resistance increased and by 1978 there were several thousand Soviet military advisers in the country. An attempt to reduce their numbers in 1978 led to a Marxist coup, in which the president was killed, and the country become even more polarised between the pro-Moscow government and rebels known as *mujaheddin* (= freedom fighters). The new president was himself killed in September 1979, but the Soviets detected a cooling in relations with the newly-installed President Amin and in December they began a covert build-up, culminating in the seizure of Kabul airport by *spetsnaz* (= special forces) units on December 24 1979. As soon as the airport was secure three airborne divisions were immediately airlifted into the country and Kabul was taken over. President Amin provided unexpected resistance, however, and in a shoot-out at the presidential palace he was killed (the third president in a row to be shot) as was the Soviet general commanding the killer squad. This event totally undermined the

ABOVE: Afghan rebel fighters, carrying captured Soviet weapons, pose aboard a captured Soviet tank on January 13 1980. Like the Americans against the Viet Cong, the Soviet army never found the right strategy and tactics to defeat the mujaheddin.

RIGHT: One weapon which the mujaheddin respected was the Soviet Mi-24 Hind gunship, which proved to be a very capable and flexible weapon system.

Soviet propaganda line that they were moving into the country in response to an invitation from the president.

Astonishingly, the Soviets repeated virtually every mistake made by the USA in the Vietnam War: they relied on vastly superior technology; moved in aircraft (particularly helicopters) wherever possible; and concentrated on holding ground and controlling facilities, such as airfields and towns. The Soviet plan of campaign was to establish garrisons in towns, clear the roads, drive the *mujaheddin* into the hills, cut the supply route from Pakistan and finally to eliminate the rebels altogether. The Soviets even had an advantage not enjoyed by the US in Vietnam in that the *mujaheddin* were riven by tribal and religious differences, and thus operated in autonomous groups. Only in 1985 was this partially overcome with several (but not all) of the groups agreeing on a common anti-Soviet strategy.

The Soviet plan must have looked good on paper, but it never worked out that way. Soviet casualties escalated, the conscripts became increasingly disaffected, and the garrison's size increased steadily, reaching well over 100,000 by 1985. For the Soviet soldiers conditions in Afghanistan were harsh, the enemy was elusive and cruel (even by Soviet standards) to prisoners, morale was low, and there was little support for the war at home in the USSR. The Mil Mi-24 Hind attack helicopter became the symbol of Soviet oppression, and there were widespread allegations of the use of chemical,

biological and biochemical weapons.

The rebels found sanctuary with their Muslim co-religionists in Pakistan where they obtained supplies and weapons, much of which came from US stocks. Peshawar, Pakistan, was also the scene of the 1986 meeting where seven *mujaheddin* groups managed, at last, to agree on a common approach to the war. By 1988 the Soviet Union, which by then was achieving rapprochement with the West in Europe, decided to pull out of Afghanistan. This started in May 1988 and was completed in February 1989. The Soviet campaign in Afghanistan was a failure, although their departure did not result in peace, but in a protracted civil war, which has continued into the late 1990s.

The Afghan War reinforced a lesson taught by the US campaign in Vietnam: there are limits to use of military might by a Superpower. The Gulf War showed that an all-embracing coalition can force a rogue state to behave in accordance with international conventions, but it is a different matter to intervene in a domestic dispute. The dilemma is that if the Superpower used all the weapons at its disposal it will be able to subjugate its opponents by sheer force, but it will undoubtedly lose the war politically.

ABOVE: Afghan villagers view an unexploded Soviet bomb. Such unexploded weapons and mines leave a terrible legacy, inflicting casualties on local people long after the war has ended and the soldiers and airmen have gone home.

Falklands War 1982

Background

The Falklands War of 1982 had its origins in the dispute between Argentina and Britain over sovereignty of the Falkland Islands in the south Atlantic. This had been rumbling on for many years when the domestic situation in Argentina, coupled with what appeared to be a surreptitious go-ahead signal from the United States, led the Argentine President, General Galtieri, to instruct his armed forces to 'recover' what the Argentinians called the Malvinas Islands.

Invasion

The Argentine invasion force, composed of some 2,000 marines, landed near Port Stanley on April 2 1982 and quickly overwhelmed the 84-strong British Royal Marine garrison, and a

ABOVE: An Argentine Marine amphibious personnel carrier halts on the waterfront in Port Stanley, capital of the Falkland Islands (Malvinas), with the Anglican cathedral in the background.

separate force captured the 22-man garrison on the island of South Georgia the next day. The British reacted very strongly and a naval task force sailed, amid great publicity, on April 5. Both the Falkland Islands and South Georgia were very remote, but the British had an incalculable asset in Ascension Island, a small island of volcanic ash in the central South Atlantic, which served as an advance base for the task force.

Recapture

As early as April 18 the first British special forces landed on the Falkland Islands to commence reconnaissances. Attention then switched to South Georgia, however, where on April 25 Royal Navy helicopters so damaged an Argentine submarine that it had to beach itself, and the next day Royal Marines and Special Air Service (SAS) troops landed at Grytviken and Leith, forcing the Argentine troops to surrender.

Britain imposed a 200 nautical mile (35km) exclusion zone around the Falkland Islands on April 28 and on May 1 aircraft from the task force started to bomb targets in the Port Stanley area. The conflict then escalated when the elderly Argentine cruiser, *General Belgrano*, was sunk with the loss of 368 lives on May 2 by

the nuclear submarine *Conqueror*, using a conventional torpedo. On May 4, however, the Argentine Navy scored an even more spectacular success by so seriously damaging the British destroyer, HMS *Sheffield*, that it had to be scuttled. In a move which was later identified as in preparation for the landings, the SAS raided Pebble Island, where they destroyed 11 Argentine aircraft and numerous base facilities.

On May 21 the British 3 Commando Brigade landed at San Carlos at the western end of East Falkland Island, confounding the Argentine commander who had expected a landing in the area of Port Stanley. The build-up ashore appeared to take a long time and strong political pressure from London forced the commander in the Falklands to undertake an operation to the south of San Carlos to capture the settlement of Goose Green. This was carried out by 2nd Battalion, Parachute Regiment (2 Para) and culminated in an attack by the British battalion group on an Argentine force of some 1,250 men. In a bitterly fought, day-long battle the British eventually succeeded, but the cost was relatively high on both sides, with the Argentines losing 250 killed and 121 wounded, while the smaller British force lost 17 killed (including the battalion's commanding officer) and 31 wounded. All Argentine survivors were captured.

Meanwhile, the remaining troops of 3 Commando Brigade had set off on foot along the northern route to Port Stanley while 5 Infantry Brigade had landed at San Carlos. By June 11 the British had pushed the Argentine troops back to the eastern end of the island and a series of successful attacks on the night of June 13/14 left the Argentine garrison penned

LEFT: The British campaign to retake the Falklands was not without pain; a number of ships were sunk including this Type 42 destroyer, HMS *Coventry*.

inside Port Stanley. The commander, General Menendez, surrendered.

Lessons

The British were not expecting to fight in the Falkland Islands and the campaign was mounted at short notice and at a distance of some 8,000 miles (12,800km) from the British Isles. Unlike at Suez, however, the action was mounted quickly and with clear determination, and neither national nor international opposition to the campaign ever became significant. The Argentinian

forces and people at home became demoralised.

Conditions on the Falklands were particularly severe and the British advance was constrained by the early loss of most of its helicopters aboard the merchant ship *Atlantic Conveyor*. Many new weapons were tested in action for the first time. The main lessons, however, were learned by the navies of the world (not just by the British) with the effectiveness of sea-skimming missiles and the vulnerability of modern warships to these weapons being demonstrated for all to see.

BELOW: Men of the British 3rd Parachute Battalion search Argentine prisoners-of-war just outside Port Stanley at the end of the campaign.

CIVIL WARS

Civil wars have been one of the major blights of the 20th Century, where sizeable elements of population have taken up arms against the remainder, either to take over the government or to seek independence for a geographically or ethnically identifiable element of the country. The major characteristics of these wars have been the bitterness with which they have been fought, increasing interference from outside, the ready availability of weapons and equipment on international markets and, in many cases, the long legacy of bitterness and mistrust they have left behind.

Russian Civil War 1917-1922

Imperial Russia suffered greatly during the first four years of the First World War, and civil and military unrest led to the overthrow of the Tsar in March 1917, with a new government being set up headed by Kerensky. This government sought to continue the war, but suffered major setbacks, leading to the Bolshevik revolution in November 1917. A new government, led by Lenin, signed an armistice with the Germans at Brest-Litovsk in December 1917, enabling the Bolsheviks to turn to domestic problems, of which there were many. Of greatest immediate importance were the civil war against the White Russians and the interference by foreign powers, including America, Britain, France and Japan.

Every now and then a rogue element appears in a conflict, an entirely random involvement by an unexpected person or group. In this case it was the so-called Czech Legion, composed of some 100,000 Bohemian soldiers of the Austria-Hungarian army who had been cap-

tured between 1914 and 1917 and sent to prisoner-of-war camps in Siberia. After the Brest-Litovsk armistice had been signed these men were promised that they would be moved by land to Vladivostok and thence by sea back home to Europe. The Soviets reneged on this deal, so the men captured arms, formed themselves into units and marched westwards along the Trans-Siberian railway. Having captured Sverdlovsk they allied themselves with troops commanded by Admiral Kolchack, who was seeking to oust the Bolsheviks, but after some initial successes Kolchack's army was pushed back by the Bolsheviks. Kolchack was captured and shot by the Bolsheviks, so the Czechs turned eastwards once again, overwhelming any opposition from either Red or White Russians that attempted to bar their way. Meanwhile a US divisional-size force had been sent to Vladivostok in August 1918 to rescue the Czech Legion (and also to prevent the

BELOW: Gunners of the newly-created Red Army under training. During the first few years of the new Communist state it was involved in many conflicts, both national and international, but by the mid-1920s the new regime was secure.

LEFT: Determined sentries pose outside the headquarters of the revolutionary movement in the Smolny Institute, St Petersburg (Petrograd) in October 1917.

LEFT: Cavalry, such as this Red Army Cossack unit, was widely used in the Civil War.

Japanese from taking over too much Russian territory). The American force held the Trans-Siberian Railway from Lake Baikal to Vladivostok until the Czechs joined up with them in late 1919.

An American, British, French intervention force was also sent to Murmansk in North-West Russia in June 1918, with the stated aim of reclaiming war supplies sent to Imperial Russia, although the covert mission was to conquer Russia and return it to Imperial rule, partly by linking up with the Czech Legion. The whole thing was a farce, with a division-sized force expected to succeed where Napoleon's huge armies had failed, and the US contingent departed in August 1919, followed by the British and French a month later.

In the end, all that was achieved by Allied interference in the Russian civil war was to create a mistrust of the West which persisted for many years. The White Russian opposition to the Communists was disjointed and reactionary, seeking simply to restore the old order without proposing plans for correcting the abuses.

Trotsky, the Bolshevik's military master-mind, had found himself facing Kolchack coming from the east, four armies in the south, a fifth on the Baltic coast, and the Allies in Archangel. Deeming Kolchack to pose the most immediate threat, Tukhachevskiy was sent eastwards, where he first stopped and then turned back the admiral, who was subsequently captured and shot. Having disposed of that threat, Tukhachevskiy headed westwards again, rolling up the four southern White Russian armies as he went. The last to be defeated was Wrangel whose forces were evacuated from the Crimea in November 1920.

ABOVE: Soldiers of the Eighth Route Army of the People's Liberation Army fighting against Chiang Kai Shek's Kuo Min-tang forces.

Chinese Civil War 1927-1949

The Chinese people suffered a long period of unrest from 1912, when the last Manchu emperor abdicated, to 1949 when the Chinese Communist Party (CCP) took power. It can be broken down into six periods:

1912-1916. Brief period of rule by President Yuan
1916-1926. The era of the 'Warlords'.
1925-1927. Revolutionary period; rise of Chiang Kai Shek.
1927-1936. Rule of Kuo Min Tang; rise of the Communist Party; 'long march'; civil war commences on August 1 1927.
1937-1945. Sino-Japanese War; Second World War.
1945-1949. Final fight for supremacy between Kuo Min Tang and CCP; People's Republic proclaimed October 1, 1949.

The young CCP carried out three unsuccessful uprisings in 1927, of which the first (at Nanchang in Kiangsi Province, August 1 1927) is now celebrated in China as the birthday of the People's Liberation Army (PLA) and is also generally taken as being the start of the civil war between the Kuo Mintang (KMT) and the

CCP. All three uprisings were based on the urban proletariat and with their failure the emphasis changed to the rural peasants.

Chiang consolidated his power from 1928 onwards and in 1930 launched a 'bandit extermination' campaign against the 'communist republic' which had been established with its capital at Juichin. The KMT forces, advised by German General von Seekt, threatened the PLA with almost certain defeat and on October 15 1934 the army set out on the 'Long March'. Accurate numbers will never be known, but approximately 100,000 started on this great undertaking of whom some 20,000 completed the entire 6,000 miles (9,600km) in November 1936, having covered some very rough terrain and fought numerous military actions on the way. In addition to these, however, a large number of men and women were dropped off on the way to foment revolution, while many others joined, inspired by the Communist determinations. This was one of the military epics of the Twentieth Century, and for speed, length and endurance has seldom been equalled in history.

During the Sino-Japanese War (see page 62) the KMT and CCP formed a 'united front' against the Japanese invaders, although, in reality, it was more of a stand-off. The CCP steadily extended its control – both military and political – of the countryside in northern and central China, emphasising discipline and honesty, while the KMT became more corrupt and its organisation began to break down. When the Japanese suddenly surrendered in August 1945 the two Chinese factions took up their civil war once more, even though President Truman despatched the prestigious General Marshall (US Army Chief of Staff throughout the war) to seek a compromise between the two sides.

The final phase of the civil war began in July 1946, with some three million Nationalist troops opposed to approximately one million in the PLA. The US gave considerable assistance to the Nationalists, short of committing troops. Chiang Kai Shek's strategy was to establish a corridor between the Yangtze and Peking, and then push the PLA back into the west and out of the war. The PLA, on the other hand, sought to expand across China from Shensi to the sea and then push northwards, while simultaneously taking Manchuria and then driving south. PLA operations in Manchuria culminated in taking Mukden in November 1948.

In Central China fortunes varied for a time; in March 1947, for example, the Nationalists succeeded in taking the Communist capital at Yenan, although Mao Tse-tung refused to call on other troops to defend the city. From then onwards the PLA gained constantly, scoring one success after another. At the Battle of the Hwai

River, General Chen Yi, commanding two PLA armies attacked two Nationalist armies, each side deploying approximately half-a-million troops. The operation lasted from November 1948 to January 1949 and was a disaster for the Nationalists who lost approximately 250,000 men, including both army commanders. The Communists took Peking on January 22 1949 and, having rejected a Nationalist offer to split the country into two, they attacked southwards from the Yangtze. Nanking fell in April 1949, Canton in October, and Chungking in November, forcing the Nationalists to move to Formosa (Taiwan), although they did manage to hold on to several small offshore islands, which have proved contentious ever since.

ABOVE: In most civil wars and revolutions it is the civilian population that tends to suffer the most. Here soldiers shoot prisoners on a river bank in China.

LEFT: Victory after more than 25 years of fighting as troops of the Chinese People's Liberation Army drive into Peking on January 31 1949, watched by curious onlookers.

ABOVE: Many outsiders interfered in the Spanish Civil War, often in order to try out their new weapons, such as this Heinkel He-111 bomber of the German Condor Legion. Such operations helped to develop techniques which were used in the first years of World War Two.

BACKGROUND PICTURE: A patrol of Franco's troops advance through damaged Santander on August 27 1937.

Spanish Civil War 1936-1939

Spain was riven by civil unrest in the early 1930s, with ever stronger animosity between the right wing (Nationalist (Falange)), centred on the army, and the left wing, which was composed of an alliance of socialists, communists and anarchists. The left-wing coalition won the national elections in February 1936, but when a military rebellion started on July 18 1936 the country split into two. General Franco, at that time one of several generals at the head of the military forces, supervised an airlift of troops (the first strategic move by air) from Melilla to mainland Spain and then marched towards Madrid.

International involvement was rapid. The Soviet Union led with support to the Loyalist (left-wing) forces, including military supplies, training teams and six 'International brigades' formed from some 30,000-plus American, British, Czech, French, German, Italian, Polish and other left-wing volunteers. The Nationalist forces were supported by formed units from Nazi Germany and Fascist Italy. France, the UK and the USA formed a non-intervention committee, in which some 30 nations (including Germany and Italy) sought to prevent the war spreading outside the Iberian peninsula, and set up a naval patrol which operated along the Spanish coast.

The capital, Madrid, was of considerable significance, with the Falangists starting the siege in November 1936, which was to last, with varying degrees of intensity, for the rest of the war. There was considerable activity elsewhere, however, with the Falangists soon controlling much of central Spain and all of Spain's Mediterranean seaboard. They had taken most of the North coast by September and by the end of the year had taken virtually the whole of the north-west, opening the ports to much-needed supplies. One of the most notorious air raids of the century took place on April 25 1936 when German *Luftwaffe* aircraft bombed the small town of Guernica, an attack given widespread publicity around the world and which appeared to add weight to the prevailing theories of air power.

The war dragged on through 1937 and 1938, with much bravery and great violence being displayed by both sides. By late 1938, however, the end was in sight, with the final Nationalist offensives starting in December 1938. France and the UK recognised the Franco government in February 1939 and the last Loyalist troops surrendered in Madrid on April 1 1939. Unable to show generosity, the new government tried and executed great numbers of former Loyalist supporters, thus ensuring that the animosities engendered by the war would continue for generations.

Greek Civil War 1946–1949

Greece was occupied by Germany during the Second World War and the principal resistance was provided by the Greek Communist Party. It had been agreed between Churchill and Stalin in early 1944 that Greece lay within the British sphere of influence so that British troops occupied the country when the Germans decamped in December 1944. The British found themselves fighting ELAS, the Communist army, and defeated them, but the Communists then moved their training and supply bases across the borders into Communist Albania and Yugoslavia, and spent the period 1945-46 in recruiting, training and low-level guerrilla operations against government forces. In 1947 the communist main force (DSE) was some 23,000 strong, with an underground force (YIAFAKA) of some 50,000 and a further half-a-million or so sympathizers. In a self-defeating gesture, Greek politicians refused to allow Greek National Army units to be moved outside their own constituencies; this meant that their constituents were protected, but, almost disastrously, that the commander-in-chief could not concentrate his forces.

Greece was in the British 'sphere of influence' but the UK was in the throes of a major post-war economic crisis and handed its responsibilities over to the USA. As a result, US aid started to arrive in late 1947 and the Communists attempted to establish autonomous zones, which failed. In 1948 the DKE began a policy of murdering government supporters and abducting potential recruits – including some 10,000 children less than 10 years old – who were taken to Yugoslavia for training. In 1949 a new commander-in-chief of the national army, Papagos, was appointed, empowered (at last!) to deploy the army as he saw fit. By coincidence a new chief took command of the DKE, who decided to move on to the third, or mobile, phase of communist revolutionary warfare. This proved to have been premature, enabling the national army to inflict several defeats on the communists, whose position was made worse when Marshal Tito closed the Yugoslavian border. Meanwhile, Papagos went on to a new strategy, penning the DKE in the mountains, while the main effort was devoted to eliminating YIAFAKA, the clandestine network intended to control the civil population and to provide

BELOW: British paratroops in Athens in December 1944, where, to their dismay, they found themselves fighting the Communist ELAS guerrillas instead of Germans.

ABOVE: Despite the machine-gun, these troops are engaged in a peace-keeping operation. Soldiers of Malaya's Royal Malay Regiment serving with the United Nations in the Congo on November 21 1961, in an operation against mutinous Congolese soldiers who murdered 18 Italian airmen of the UN force.

support and intelligence for the DKE. This achieved, Papagos attacked the DKE in its main position in the Mount Vitsi area, where the communists committed the cardinal error of trying to make a stand and were, once again, defeated. The war was over by August 1949.

One of the curious features of this war was that the USSR never helped the communists and it is often speculated that this was because Stalin was standing by his 1944 undertaking to Churchill. Whatever the reason, in the post-war era when communism seemed to be gaining ground everywhere, this was a welcome success for the West.

Congo (Zaire) Civil War (Katanga revolt) 1960-1964

The colony of Belgian Congo was acquired as a personal fiefdom by King Leopold in 1885 but was later taken over by the Belgian state.

There was unrest in the country from 1949 onwards, but in 1960 the Belgians suddenly decided to grant independence at only a few months' notice. Preparations for such a move were totally inadequate, the new Congolese administrators were untrained, and the situation was made worse by a mass exodus of Europeans. The following eight years were chaotic: the government of the country changed repeatedly; various states seceded, notably the mineral-rich Katanga; murders and unexplained deaths were frequent and included former Congolese premier Lumumba (shot), former Katangese premier Tshombe ('heart failure' in Algeria) and UN Secretary-General Dag Hammerskjold (unexplained air crash). The UN became deeply embroiled in the mess, with the first troops deploying in July 1960 and the last departing in June 1964; the force peaked at some 19,000 and its involvement was both controversial and costly, and, in the end, solved nothing.

The conflict also marked the initial rise to prominence of the mercenary soldier. Hostages were frequently taken and often slain. The United States, the USSR and China were all dragged in. Among the issues were super-power rivalry, communism versus capitalism, and the vast mineral wealth of Katanga, which was predominantly owned by the Belgian company *Union Miniere*.

General Mobutu seized power in 1965 and the rest of the world was relieved to see him bring relative calm to the country, although there have been frequent upheavals since.

Nigerian Civil War 1967-1970

The British colony of Nigeria achieved independence in October 1960 and initially enjoyed relative stability, although inter-tribal

BELOW: Troops of the Federal Nigerian Army operating against rebel Biafrans, August 27 1967.

jealousies, coupled with economic and political imbalances, created tensions. In 1966, however, a military coup ousted the president, who was killed, and the new president infuriated northerners by changing the constitution from a federal to a unitary state. Colonel Gowon (a northerner) seized power in mid-1966 and in May 1967 the south-east part of Nigeria broke away, declaring itself the independent state of Biafra. The ensuing civil war lasted to 1970, with Biafra gaining a considerable degree of international support. The federal forces used their superior manpower and training gradually to isolate and then eliminate the opposition, until the rebels were finally forced to surrender in January 1970.

Irish Civil War

The histories of England and Ireland have been inextricably intertwined since the island was granted to King Henry II by the pope and English rule was established between 1167 and 1171. There were periodic uprisings over the following centuries, with particularly bloody episodes in 1649-50, 1689-1691, 1795-97, and 1916-1921. This last was the culmination of many years of unrest and broke out on Easter Sunday 1916. The British were involved in the First World War at the time and put the rising down rapidly and firmly, but rebellion returned in 1919, turning into a particularly brutal and bloody conflict, which eventually forced the British to make all of Ireland except for the province of Ulster into the Irish Free State.

Unfortunately, the continuing British presence in Protestant-dominated Ulster left a cause which could be exploited by extremists and a long period of low-level violence eventually escalated. Inter-communal feeling became so high in April 1969 that British troops had to be deployed to keep the peace. This led into a campaign of violence by the Provisional Irish Republican Army (Catholics) and by various Loyalist groups (Protestant) which has continued at varying degrees of intensity to the present day.

GREAT POWER OPERATIONS

There has been a tacit recognition throughout the 20th Century that Great Powers have a 'sphere of influence', particularly in areas close to their borders, where they may act to ensure their own security in a manner which, if done further afield, would be regarded as cause for war. Thus, the Soviet Union was able to quash revolts in the Warsaw Pact area with relative impunity, while the United States has, for many years, assumed the right to involve itself in the domestic affairs of neighbours in Central and South America. China assumes similar rights in relation to its neighbours.

Soviet Union

From 1945 to the late 1980s, the USSR maintained its hegemony over eastern Europe by military power and, apart from the routine of a widespread military occupation, there were several occasions where force was overtly used. There was serious rioting in East Berlin in June 1953, which the German Democratic Republic was unable to contain, and the Soviet Army moved in to quell it. The Western Allies protested but did nothing to counter it. Much more serious was the outbreak of a popular revolt in Hungary on October 23 1956, when an anti-Communist demonstration was violently dispersed. Nationwide protests followed, fighting broke out and the Soviet Union dithered for several days, appearing at one stage to be prepared to allow Hungary a degree of national sovereignty. Then, on October 29,

BELOW: British troops man an improvised barricade in Dublin, Ireland, during the rising on Easter Sunday 1916. The Lewis machine-gun (third from left) was an unusually powerful weapon for such an operation.

ATELY began introducing reforms, which caused considerable concern to other members of the Warsaw Pact. A formal letter of warning was sent to the Czechoslovak leadership in June, but on August 20 an overwhelming military force composed of contingents from Bulgaria, East Germany, Hungary, Poland and the Soviet Union poured across the border, swamping Czech resistance.

ABOVE: Soviet troops entering Czechoslovakia in 1968 were astonished at the opposition from the younger generation.

BELOW: US artillery shelling Cuban hiding places during the 1983 invasion of Grenada.

in an entirely unrelated move, Israel attacked the Suez Canal and the Anglo-French ultimatum to Israel and Egypt was issued (see page 47), which appears to have tipped the balance in favour of Soviet action in Hungary and, after a few days of prevarication while they deployed the necessary troops, the Soviet Union struck on November 4. The battle of Budapest lasted until November 14, but ended with the inevitable Soviet victory.

One more national uprising was to be brutally suppressed: in Czechoslovakia in 1968. Alexander Dubcek became first secretary of the Communist party in early 1968 and immedi-

United States

Fidel Castro took power in Cuba in January 1959 and soon turned to the Soviet Union for help and aid. By mid-1962 evidence was accumulating that Soviet military aid included offensive missiles, and this was soon confirmed by aerial reconnaissance. President Kennedy made the situation public on October 22 1962, announcing the imposition of a naval blockade. US forces were placed on full alert on October 22, followed by Soviet forces next day, but rapid behind-the-scenes diplomacy resulted in an agreement that Soviet missiles and bombers would be removed from Cuba. In return the USA undertook not to invade Cuba and to remove missiles from Turkey. The crisis was over by early December, but showed the determination of a superpower when its vital interests were threatened.

A totally different type of operation took place in the Caribbean island of Grenada. Maurice Bishop assumed power in a *coup d'etat* in 1979 and established close ties with both Cuba, which despatched 'construction workers' to the island, and the USSR, which sent military advisers. Bishop was deposed in

October 1983 and the island quickly descended into chaos, whereupon a group of East Caribbean states requested the USA to intervene and restore peace and order. For the USA, an additional factor was that there was a medical college on the island, where some 1,000 young Americans were under training. A 6,000-strong US force and 500 men from other Caribbean states landed on October 25 1983 in a combined airborne and amphibious operation, which was successful, despite some spirited resistance from the Cubans.

General Noriega became dictator in Panama in 1983 and by 1989 was under very heavy pressure to resign. He was indicted in the USA for drug trafficking and money laundering, and also rejected the outcome of unfavourable elections at home. Taking the killing of a US Marine as justification, the USA invaded Panama in overwhelming strength on December 20 1989. Panama City and the countryside were rapidly taken over, although Noriega did not give himself up until January 3 1990 and was then deported to the USA for trial. This particular action by the USA came in for considerable criticism.

China

China had ancient claims to Tibet and once the People's Republic had been established in 1949 Chinese leader Mao Tse-tung set about reclaiming the lost territory. The Chinese invasion took place in October 1950 and the country was quickly overrun, mainly because it did not have an army. There have been sporadic outbreaks of unrest ever since. The Dalai Lama escaped to India in 1959.

On its southern border, Chinese relations with Vietnam have not always been good, even though China provided great amounts of aid as well as an active sanctuary to the Viet Minh in the First Indochina War. In early 1979, however, relations between the two countries were so strained over Vietnam's military activities in Laos and Cambodia that China carried out a limited incursion in the mountains of the Viet Bac.

On February 17 1979, a force of some 25,000 troops and 1,200 tanks penetrated some 20 miles (32km) into Vietnamese territory, halted, paused and then withdrew back into China. The Vietnamese army put up strong resistance although it does not appear that the Chinese ever intended to advance further than they did. The whole affair was over by March 15, and it remains difficult to see what was achieved.

India

Indian independence from the United Kingdom in 1947 did not include the small enclave of Goa, which had been ruled by Portugal since the 15th Century. There were some violent clashes on the border with India in 1954-55, sparked off by Indian nationalists, which led to India breaking off diplomatic relations with Portugal. Matters rested there for several years until December 18 1961, when the Indian armed forces suddenly seized Goa in a very rapid operation. The international community was faced with a *fait accompli* and simply accepted the situation.

BELOW: Chinese tanks carry infantry across the Khi Kong River, just 80 miles (130km) northeast of Hanoi during the short-lived 1979 invasion.

OTHER CONFLICTS

RIGHT: French General Baumgarten moves his troops to occupy Taza, east of Fez, the Moroccan capital, in 1914. Much fought-over, this strip of land in North Africa was once policed jointly by France and Spain.

INSURGENCY AND INSURRECTION

Spanish Morocco 1912-1926

Morocco was an independent sultanate from the Middle Ages, but by the end of the 19th Century it was in permanent revolt against the ruler and was being targeted by France as a

potential addition to its North African Empire. These plans were temporarily thwarted by the Moroccan Crisis of 1905 when Kaiser Wilhelm II of Germany landed at Tangier and made a pro-Moroccan speech. This was resolved by an international conference held at Algeciras, Spain, where France and Spain became responsible for policing Morocco 'while respecting the authority of the Sultan'. This led in 1912 to the formal partition of Morocco between the two countries with the south becoming a French protectorate while the north went to Spain.

Trouble continued in Spanish Morocco, with Abd el Krim, leader of the Riff tribe, conducting a skilful guerrilla war. In 1921 a Spanish force of some 20,000 men set off into the Riff Mountains to deal with this threat, but the Riffs attacked first, capturing a frontier post, which caused the garrison of the next post at Anual to flee without having come under attack. They reached the advancing Spanish force on July 21 1921, bringing wild stories of the Riffs' success. Unfortunately, their arrival coincided with an ambush by another group of Riffs and the situation became confused, the Spanish command system broke down and the troops started to panic, enabling the Riffs to turn what might have been a minor success into a major victory. Some 12,000 men of the Spanish force, including the commanding general, were killed and thousands more taken prisoner.

This encouraged Abd el Krim to reorganise his force along more conventional lines, armed mainly with modern weapons, including artillery and machine guns. This took some time to achieve, but in April 1925, Abd el Krim moved south where he attacked and overran most of the defended posts on the French side of the border and was stopped only when close to the capital at Fez.

The Battle of Anual had electrified both the French and the Spanish; indeed, in the latter case it brought down the government. The two countries managed to agree on a combined campaign and the French Army in French Morocco was reinforced to a strength in excess of 150,000, while Spain despatched a new force of some 50,000 men, which landed under the protection of a joint Franco-Spanish naval force on September 8 1925. The French then

drove northwards, pushing the Riffs back on to the Spanish force which was heading south. The Riffs fought very hard, but they were faced by overwhelming strength and Abd el Krim was eventually compelled to surrender on May 26 1926.

Malayan 'Emergency' 1948-1960

During the Second World War the main internal opposition to the Japanese occupation was centred on the Malayan People's Anti-Japanese Army (MPAJA), the military arm of the Malayan Communist Party (MCP). The MCP was unable to oppose the return of the British in 1945 and cooperated for the first few years of peace, but then decided to 'go underground', the insurgency (or 'emergency' as it was euphemistically known) starting on June 16 1948. The Communist campaign was initially spread all over the country, with guerrilla gangs operating from jungle hideouts, and terrorising people in the rural areas. The government forces consisted of Australian, British and New Zealand units, with an ever-increasing

ABOVE: A terrorist is questioned by an interpreter during an operation in the Malayan state of Johore in 1951. Constant infantry operations drove the CTs to defeat in Malaya, leading to independence ('*Merdeka*') in 1957.

LEFT: Men of the British Coldstream Guards ford a river during an operation against the 'CTs' (Communist terrorists) in Malaya in 1950.

ABOVE: A British soldier with a Bren light machine-gun stands guard over a barbed-wire 'cage' full of suspects during Operation Anvil, which cleared Nairobi of Mau-Mau terrorists.

proportion of Malayan units found from both the army and the police. The enemy, the Malayan Races Liberation Army (MRLA) under the direction of the MCP, was predominantly Chinese, but with a number of Malays and Indians (and at least two Japanese), as well.

Government strategy was to sever the link between the MCP/MRLA in the jungle and the people 'outside' who provided intelligence, supplies, money and recruits. There was also a concurrent campaign to take the war into the deep jungle against the hard core of the insurgent movement. The country was progressively cleared 'white', which involved very large numbers of troops, police and auxiliaries, and took time, but in the end it was extremely successful. The British granted full independence to Malaya in August 1957 (which removed, at a stroke, one of the Communists' main propaganda aims) and the war was declared officially at an end on July 31 1960. Under pressure from the Malaysian Army, the MCP withdrew across the border into Thailand, where it held out for many years until 1990, when the final 1,200 surrendered to the government after a 'revolution' which had lasted for 41 years.

Mau-Mau Campaign (Kenya) 1953-1955

Kenya was the setting for a quite different type of insurgency in the early 1950s, which had nothing to do with Communism. The Mau-Mau movement was confined to a section of one tribe – the Kikuyu – with minor elements from two other, smaller tribes. There were a number of reasons for the uprising, including: a growing disparity in wealth and status between the white settlers and the majority black population; the large influx of new white settlers after the war; and the disillusionment among black soldiers who had enlisted in the British Army during the Second World War and returned to Kenya to resume their lowly status as peasant farmers.

As usual, it took some time for the colonial authorities to grasp the seriousness of the threat, but the 'emergency' was declared on October 20 1952. The bloodshed continued, which was aimed at whites in general and at blacks who supported the government. The government forces were reorganised and strengthened, a new headquarters was set up, and some of the more successful lessons of other counter-insurgency campaigns, particularly Malaya, brought to bear.

For the Mau-Mau, the high point of the campaign was on March 26 1953 when they carried out two simultaneous attacks, one on a village and the other on a police station. Their main guerrilla tactics were murders and small-

scale attacks, and they used particularly brutal methods against fellow Kikuyu tribesmen in an effort to cow them into supporting the movement. Their weapons were almost entirely primitive, such as knives and clubs, or home-made guns, with very short effective ranges.

The counter-insurgency campaign began to take effect in 1953, with a major success in the Aberdare forest, where more than 125 Mau-Mau were killed, and in 1954 it was in full swing. The capital city, Nairobi, was surrounded and systematically sectioned off and searched for a whole month in April 1954. Many arrests were made, cutting off a major source of intelligence and supplies for the terrorists. As in Malaya, whole villages were resettled and home guards formed to protect them. One feature of the campaign was to use 'counter-gangs' composed almost entirely of surrendered terrorists led by white officers disguised as blacks. Another tactic, especially in the highlands, was to organise very large-scale manhunts, with vast crowds of local villagers acting as 'beaters' to drive any Mau-Mau in the area towards cordons of army units.

The campaign began to wind down in 1955 and in 1961 the Mau-Mau leader, Jomo Kenyatta (who had been imprisoned in 1953) was released. Kenya became independent within the British Commonwealth in 1963 with Kenyatta as president, and the last of the Mau-Mau surrendered. The country has remained relatively stable ever since.

Algerian War 1954-1962

The French occupation of Algeria began in 1830 and in 1848 the country, which is situated opposite France on the southern shore of the Mediterranean, was absorbed into Metropolitan France as simply another *département*. This gave the opportunity for a large number of European settlers to move in, although they were by no means all of French origin; they were known as *colons* (=colonists) or, colloquially, as *pied noir* (=black feet). These *colons* enjoyed special political, financial and economical status, which exacerbated their relations with the Muslim majority. The anti-colonial movement gathered strength in the mid-1940s and by 1954 the *Front de Libération Nationale* (FLN) was ready to launch the opening strike of its campaign on November 1 1954.

Following its defeat in Indo-China (see page 63), the French Army had made a detailed and thorough study of revolutionary warfare and proceeded to apply the lessons to this new campaign, with a considerable degree of success. The army took immediate and positive action, making serious inroads into FLN numbers and organisation, but without actually destroying it. The FLN recovered and on August 20 1955 it massacred some 120 *colons* in villages around Philippeville, but a ferocious retaliation by the *colons* resulted in approximately 12,000 Muslim deaths. Then, in March 1956, France gave independence to the adjacent territories of Morocco and Tunisia, which not only created friendly borders beyond which the FLN could train, organise and find shelter, but also gave yet another spur to the concept of independence.

Meanwhile, the FLN had created a substantial organisation in the capital city, Algiers, which started a campaign of bombing and assassination in 1957. Unable to cope, the authorities handed complete control to the French Army's 10th Parachute Division and in the ensuing 'Battle of Algiers' *les paras* totally wiped out the FLN organisation in the city. The methods they used, however, while militarily effective, involved not only torture but also numerous 'disappearances', which had severe political repercussions in Metropolitan France, as a result of which support for the campaign dropped.

Meanwhile, the French solved the problem of the Tunisian sanctuary by constructing a

BELOW: Tanks deploy to protect Paris from invasion by disaffected paratroops, also French, from Algeria.

very long barrier, just inside French territory, known as the 'Morice' line. The main barrier was a nine strand 8ft (2.5m) high wire fence carrying a 5,000 volt charge, with dense anti-personnel minefields on both sides, and a constantly patrolled track 165ft (50m) inside the fence. An elaborate system of alarms was backed by some 80,000 rapid response troops, but despite the expense (and unlike many other so-called barriers) it proved highly effective and virtually isolated the many FLN elements in Tunisia from Algeria. The FLN endeavoured to penetrate the line in the winter of 1957-58 and failed, incurring very heavy losses. A similar fence was built on the Moroccan border.

When it became obvious that the Army was winning the military battle but losing the political one, elements in the French Army began to seek a political solution. In addition, the *colons* were becoming increasingly dissatisfied with support from successive weak French governments and in May 1958 a series of public demonstrations by *colons* in Algiers, coupled with threats of military intervention in Paris, led to the collapse of the Fourth Republic and the return of De Gaulle to power as president. De Gaulle's attitude to *Algerie Francaise* was ambivalent, to say the least, and eventually elements of the French military in Algeria organised an attempt, headed by four generals, to take over power, first in Algeria and subsequently in France. Although the French government headed by De Gaulle appeared vulnerable for several days, the coup eventually proved to be a complete failure and the leadership was totally outwitted by De Gaulle. The long and bitter struggle ended with Algeria achieving complete independence on July 3 1962. The *colons* were given no special rights in the new country and emigrated to France in vast numbers.

The Algerian War was typical of a certain type of colonial insurgency in which there were three elements: the government; the indigenous population seeking independence; and European settlers. The French Army's post-Indochina study of revolutionary war was very effective and there is no doubt that they achieved a major military success over the FLN. However, a variety of factors, including the intransigent attitude of the *colons* towards the Muslims, the declining support for the war at home, and the counter-productive use of torture and assassination, meant that the military success was never turned into a political one.

Cyprus (EOKA) 1963-1967

Cyprus was captured from the Venetians by the Turks in 1571, and they allowed the English to station a small garrison on the island from 1878. The British annexed Cyprus in 1914 and

made it a Crown Colony in 1925. The population was (and remains) approximately 80 per cent Greek and 18 per cent Turkish, and the former constantly called for *Enossis* (=union with Greece), although the island has never in its history been part of Greece. The Turkish Cypriots demanded that it should either be returned to Turkey or partitioned.

There were serious riots by Greek Cypriots in 1931, which were quelled, but in the early 1950s an armed movement called EOKA (National Organisation of Greek Fighters) was formed to obtain *Enossis*, led by Colonel Grivas, a former Greek Army officer of Greek

LEFT: French paras in the casbah during the 1957 Battle of Algiers. The battle was won, but the French lost the war.

BELOW: A hazard of peacekeeping; a UN soldier is taken into custody by an irregular in Cyprus in 1964.

ABOVE: Greek Cypriots shelter behind sand-bags as they keep watch over a Turkish-Cypriot area in the island's capital, Nicosia, in 1963. The island is still partitioned and no solution is yet in sight.

Cypriot origin. The struggle which took place between 1954 and 1959 was a three-way affair, involving the British, the Greek Cypriots and the Turkish Cypriots, with the latter two being supported by the Greek and Turkish national governments, respectively. EOKA started the campaign with a hard-core strength of approximately 100 and ended with some 300, but it had widespread sympathy among the Greek Cypriot community and created trouble out of all proportion to its numbers, until the British tired of the struggle. The methods used were small-scale attacks on British servicemen and facilities and, at least initially, limited attacks on Turkish-Cypriots, together with riots, boycotts, strikes and outbreaks of civil disobedience. The campaign was under the clandestine leadership of Greek-Orthodox Archbishop Makarios, who was exiled to the Seychelles Islands, although, contrary to British expectations, this had little effect on the conduct of the campaign.

The outcome of the campaign was something nobody involved had either anticipated or fought for, which was complete independence for the island as a unitary state, with guaranteed rights for the Turkish Cypriot minority. This was achieved in 1959, with Makarios as the first president. The subsequent history of the island has shown how intractable such problems can be, as intercommunal violence led to a United Nations force being deployed there in 1964, while Turkey invaded the island in 1974 and maintains a military presence in Cyprus to this day.

Southern Rhodesia 1964-1979

The insurgency in Southern Rhodesia, which lasted from 1964 to 1979, was, in effect, a four-way conflict, involving the colonial power (Britain), the white settlers, and two guerrilla movements, which were split on tribal lines and unable to agree on almost anything. Southern Rhodesia was originally a Crown Colony, with the white settlers being given a large degree of autonomy in 1923; this was intended to enable them to run the affairs of the settlers (ca 23,000), but they rapidly assumed the power to govern the blacks (ca 1,000,000), as well. In 1953 the British sought to form a politically and ethnically balanced entity to which they could eventually give full independence by amalgamating the territories of Northern Rhodesia, Southern Rhodesia and Nyasaland into the Central African Federation, a move which was very unpopular with the blacks, who formed their first nationalist movement in 1957. Trouble increased and in 1962 the right wing Rhodesian Front gained power in Southern Rhodesia, leading two years later to the collapse of the Central African Federation. Northern Rhodesia became Zambia and Nyasaland became Malawi, both under black governments, while Southern Rhodesia, became Rhodesia, but remained under white minority rule.

Ian Smith, prime minister of Southern Rhodesia, sought independence from Britain, which Britain was prepared to grant only if there were specific safeguards for the black population. Disagreement culminated in Smith making a 'unilateral declaration of independence' (UDI) in November 1965. Sanctions were imposed, first by the British and later by the UN, although for many years these were ineffective, as supplies continued to reach the country via South Africa and Mozambique.

Black opposition to Smith's regime came from two movements, the Zimbabwe African National Union (ZANU) and the Zimbabwe African People's Union (ZAPU); both operated from Zambian territory but were completely independent of each other.

Early guerrilla operations were unsuccessful and it was not until 1973/74 that they became a significant factor, especially after a black government had assumed power in the former Portuguese territory of Mozambique in 1974. Then South Africa disengaged in order to concentrate on its problems at home. Talks were held in Geneva to end the conflict, but ZAPU and ZANU were unable to agree on anything, which led to Smith reaching an 'internal settlement' with a black Methodist cleric, Bishop Muzorewa, who became Prime Minister in March 1978. These manoeuvrings spurred the guerrillas to greater efforts despite powerful raids by the Security Forces against their bases, particularly in Mozambique. The two guerrilla movements were given considerable outside support, and in their base areas were large training camps, many of whose staff were Warsaw Pact instructors.

By now, large areas of Rhodesia were under virtually permanent guerrilla control and the

ABOVE: Rhodesian troops search an African hut during the war which resulted from the white Rhodesians' Unilateral Declaration of Independence (UDI).

LEFT: A Rhodesian train lies on its side, having been blown off the rails by a rebel explosion. No one such incident causes defeat, but the sum of an endless series of such events can eventually cause a government to collapse.

situation inside the country steadily deteriorated. The British government seized this opportunity to propose a new solution, which the Rhodesian government had little choice but to accept. The country was taken under direct British rule, a British governor was installed, a Commonwealth force was sent in to assemble the two guerrilla armies and a 'one man-one vote' election was held, which resulted in a black-dominated government led by Robert Mugabe taking power in March 1980.

Portuguese Guinea, the insurgency started in 1959 with government troops firing on strikers, killing 50. The PAIGC, operating from bases in Senegal and the Congo Republic, opened its campaign in 1963 and by 1970 was in control of approximately 50 per cent of the country. A new Portuguese commander, General Spinola, was more successful than his predecessors and by 1973 the campaign was at a stalemate.

The population of Angola had watched

ABOVE: Mozambique freedom fighters start their military training in Tanzania with arms drill, using sticks instead of rifles. Many freedom movements started with such scenes and ended with the defeat of the government.

Insurgencies in Portuguese African territories 1963-1974

Portugal was the first European power to colonise Africa, and possessed three territories – Angola, Guinea and Mozambique – which in 1951 were declared overseas provinces, electing members direct to the Portuguese parliament, although the franchise was by no means universal. Independence movements in all three territories were formed in 1956. In Mozambique there was *Frente de Libertacao de Mozambique* (FRELIMO) and in Guinea *Partido Africano da Independencia da Guiné e Cabo Verde* (PAIGC). Angola had three separate movements: *Movimento Popular de Libertacao de Angola* (MPLA); *Frente Nacional de Libertacao de Angola* (FNLA); and the *Uniao Nacional Para a Independencia Total de Angola* (UNITA).

In the smallest of these territories,

events in the neighbouring Congo (see page 86) with both interest and alarm, and there was a series of anti-government incidents in the late 1950s, culminating in a revolt in the northern province in March 1961. Taken by surprise, the Portuguese responded with a mixture of firm military action coupled with concessions aimed at removing the differences between Portuguese citizens of European and African stock. All three guerrilla movements had active sanctuaries in neighbouring territories and although they kept up the pressure on the Portuguese forces they seldom had more than 25 per cent of their force inside Angola. In Mozambique, FRELIMO was approximately 8,000 strong by 1971 and maintained sporadic attacks against the Portuguese. They made special efforts to threaten the huge Cabora-Basso dam project, but never actually brought work to a standstill.

The load of all these wars was more than

Portugal could sustain. In 1974 134,000 troops were deployed in the three African territories (Angola – 57,000; Mozambique – 50,000; and Portuguese Guinea – 27,000) while cumulative losses were 11,000 killed and 30,000 wounded. Nor was the political situation in Portugal healthy and a military *coup d'etat* in April 1974 resulted in a new government, which moved very rapidly to disengage from Africa. Portuguese Guinea achieved its independence in September 1974, followed by Mozambique in June 1975. Angola was made independent in November 1975, but the existence of the three separate movements, quickly led to a civil war which continued for many years.

ABOVE: Portuguese infantry soldiers in action against FNLA guerrillas in Angola in August 1961.

BELOW: An often-used trap - a trench covered by palm fronds - is avoided by Portuguese troops in Angola.

The Wars in the former Yugoslavia

The final conflict to be mentioned is perhaps not only the most dangerous but also the most indefinable of all, since it contains elements of war between newly-independent states and thus 'international' as well as internal conflicts more correctly categorised as insurgency or civil war. Numerous external bodies have become involved as they have sought to negotiate between the parties; such bodies have included the UN, the European Union, the North Atlantic Treaty Organisation, and *ad hoc* negotiating teams, such as the 'Contact Group'. In addition, a variety of international armed forces groups have deployed on behalf of the UN and NATO in an endeavour to keep the peace. Not surprisingly, the almost ceaseless political manoeuvring and frequent realignments have presented a bewildering picture to those not directly involved.

At the beginning of the 20th Century, the northern part of the area (Bosnia-Herzegovina, Croatia and Slovenia) was part of the Austria-Hungarian Empire, while the two southern states of Montenegro and Serbia were independent, having obtained their freedom from the

Ottoman Empire in 1799 and 1878, respectively. All five were united in 1918 as the 'Kingdom of Serbs, Croats and Slovenes' although this awkward title was changed to Yugoslavia (=state of southern Slavs) in 1929. During the Second World War the country was occupied by the Germans, who were resisted by two guerrilla groups: the Serbian Chetniks and the Communist Partisans, the latter being led by Marshal Tito. After the war Tito seized power and imposed a strong central government, but with some powers delegated to the 'republics' of Bosnia-Herzegovina, Croatia, Macedonia, Montenegro, Serbia and Slovenia, together with two autonomous provinces of Kosovo and Vojvodina. Although these republics were based on ethnic divisions, virtually all of them contained substantial minorities from other ethnic groups, a factor of little importance while the state of Yugoslavia remained in being.

After Tito's death in 1980, this explosive mixture held together for a while, but matters came to a head when Slovenia and Croatia declared their independence in June 1991, following which the Krajina Serbs declared themselves independent of Croatia in January 1991.

BELOW: A Yugoslav Federal Army M-84 tank stands guard in a Serbian enclave in Croatia, but most engagements in the vicious conflicts in the former Yugoslavia have been fought with much less sophisticated weapons.

Savage fighting erupted in May 1991 and a United Nations Protection Force (UNPRO-FOR 1) was deployed, which reduced but did not eliminate the fighting.

Bosnia was made up of Muslims (40 per cent), Serbs (31 per cent) and Croats (17 per cent) and the majority leader, Izetbegovic, held a referendum in early 1992; the Muslims and Croats voted for independence, but the Serbs, who were only interested in union with Serbia, boycotted it. Following the referendum, Izetbegovic declared independence in April 1992, which was recognised by the international community, but led immediately to outbreaks of violence throughout the country. This was the period of the notorious 'ethnic cleansing' and led to the deployment of UNPROFOR 2, which was responsible for humanitarian support, keeping supply routes open, monitoring ceasefire agreements and deterring attacks on the UN-declared safe areas. Fighting in Bosnia continued throughout 1993 and by August 1994 the Bosnian Serbs controlled some 70 per cent of the country. The Bosnian Serbs received arms and support from Serbia until August 1994 when this aid was cut off by President Milosevic.

LEFT: Two Serbs run for shelter during a street battle with Muslims in Safna on April 29 1992.

BELOW: Federal Yugoslav Army troops in a battle with Croatian forces in the town of Vukovar in 1991.

FAR RIGHT: One of the almost ceaseless military activities around the world is the *coup d'etat.* Here a rebel (in camouflage fatigues) surrenders after an attempted coup in Bangkok, Thailand.

RIGHT: Among the legacies of the many conflicts of the 20th Century are millions of anti-personnel mines, which continue to claim innocent civilian victims for many years after the conflict has ended and the troops have dispersed. Here Bosnian troops begin to clear 2,000 mines north of Tuzla, December 19 1995.

Macedonia had become part of the Serb-led Federal Republic of Yugoslavia in April 1992, but obtained full independence in 1993, despite Greek reservations. In 1995 the USA brokered a peace agreement at Dayton, Ohio, which was initialled on November 21 and led to the deployment of the NATO-led IFOR.

The various countries of the former Yugoslavia were relatively peaceful in the period following the Dayton accords, but renewed violence seems highly probable, not least because, despite the horrors of 'ethnic cleansing', sizeable minorities exist in many areas. Indeed, as the sudden collapse of law and order in Albania in early 1997 showed, the potential for violence seems to be ever-present throughout the Balkans.

It may appear that there is nothing beneficial about this appalling series of conflicts. However, it was extremely fortunate that the collapse of Yugoslavia occurred after the end of the Cold War since, had it happened in the 1960s or 1970s, the two Superpowers could not have avoided becoming embroiled in the events and confrontation would have been almost inevitable, possibly leading to war. Secondly, the fielding of military forces by NATO has been a major step-forward in peacekeeping, principally because NATO, alone among the international bodies, can deploy a fully-functioning command, control and communications system. Thirdly, the various forces have included components from Russia, a number of other Eastern European countries, and also from countries outside Europe, such as Malaysia.

Other minor wars

There have been numerous other minor wars extending over the entire century. These include insurrections against the colonial power, such as the Druze rebellion in Lebanon (1935-36); and the Indonesian campaign against the Dutch (1945-48). The years 1946-1980 saw a particular phenomenon of Communist Revolutionary Warfare, in which Communist-inspired movements sought to take power either from colonial powers or from indigenous governments. Such campaigns took place in Cuba (1957-59); Nicaragua (1975-79); Peru (1978-91); Philippines (1946-54 and 1964-74); and

Thailand (1975-76). Perhaps the most curious war of all took place between El Salvador and Honduras in June 1969, which arose from disputes over the outcome of a football match.

BELOW: Nicaraguan Contra sentries with a Soviet heavy machine-gun captured from the Sandinistas.

TERRORISM/COUNTER-TERRORISM

Terrorism is the use of premeditated, politically-motivated violence against military or non-combatant targets and has been used for hundreds of years, but in the 20th Century it has become a serious international problem. There are three major varieties:

Autonomous terrorists, who form small, independent groups, espousing an extreme cause, which is unlikely to achieve significant popular support, and who resort to violence to gain publicity and recruits.

A SELECTION OF TERRORIST MOVEMENTS KNOWN TO BE OPERATIONAL 1980s-1990s[1]

Organisation[2]	Estimated hard core member-ship	HQ	Aims	Typical incidents	Remarks
Abu Nidal	500	Libya	Armed struggle against Zionist enemy; undermine Israeli-Palestinian rapprochement	Murder (especially diplomats); hi-jack airliners; hotel attacks.	
15 May	Small	?	Destroy Israel.	Bombs in buildings and airliners.	a. Split from PFLP in late 1970s b. Name marks foundation of Israel: May 15 1947.
Democratic Front for Liberation of Palestine (DFLP)	500	?	Revolutionary change in Arab countries, especially monarchies as prelude to success of Palestinian struggle.	Bombs, grenades, small scale military attacks (eg. on buses).	
Fatah	11,000	Tunisia	Independent, secular Palestinian state.	Assassination, hi-jacking.	Murdered Israeli athletes at Munich Olympics 1972.
Hizballah (Islamic Jihad)	3,000+	Lebanon	Establish Sh'ia states in Lebanon, Palestine.	Suicide car bombs, murder, kidnap, hi-jack.	
Palestine Liberation Front	300	?	Independent Palestinian state.	Attacks in Israel, hi-jacked ship Achille Lauro.	Have used hot air balloons and hang gliders.
Popular Front for Liberation of Palestine (PFLP)	1,000	?	Marxist/Leninist Palestinian state.	Hi-jacking airliners; bus attacks in Israel.	
Basque Fatherland and Liberty (ETA)	200	Spain	Independent Basque state.	Bombs, kidnaps, rocket attacks, car bombs.	
Irish National Liberation Army (INLA)	?	Ireland	Unification of Ireland under 'socialist' government.	Bombs, car bombs, murder.	Military arm of Irish Republican Socialist Party.
Provisional Irish Republican Army (PIRA)	2-400	Ireland	Unification of Ireland under 'socialist' government.	Shooting, bombing, mortar attacks.	Extensive links with other terrorist organisations.
Red Army Faction (RAF)	20-30	Germany	Destroy Western capitalism.	Bombs, kidnaps, grenades.	Also known as 'Bader-Meinhoff Gang'
Red Brigades	50-75	Italy	Destroy Italian government.	Murder, kidnaps.	
Bandera Roja (Red Flag)	>50	?	Dictatorship of Proletariat in Venezuela.	Robbery, murder.	
Popular Liberation Movement (MPL)	>200	Honduras	Marxist-Leninist	Bombing, hostages.	Also known as Cinchoneros.
Farabundo Marti National Liberation Front (FMLN)	7,500	El Salvador	Leftist government in El Salvador.	Shooting, grenades, murder.	
19th April Movement (M-19)	1,000	Colombia	People's struggle against 'bourgeoisie' & US imperialism.	Kidnapping, hi-jacking armed attacks.	
Sendero Luminoso (Shining Path)	5,000	Peru	Undertake peasant armed struggle to install leftist Indian state by 2000.	Bombs, murder.	Chief was captured, imprisoned in 1992
Tupac Amaru	200	Peru	Destabilise Peruvian government; expel US influences	Shooting, bombs, murder, kidnap.	Captured Japanese embassy, December 1996.
Chukaku Ha	3,000	Japan	Abolish current government & monarchy; remove US forces.	Flamethrower, mortar, bombs, rockets.	
Liberation Tigers of Tamil Belam	2,000	Sri Lanka	Separate Tamil state in North East Sri Lanka.	Bombs, mortars, ambush, murder.	Also known as Tamil Tigers.

[1] Source: 'Terrorist Group Profiles' US Government Printing Office, 1989.
[2] This was the situation in 1988; some of these groups are now dormant and new groups may have appeared since this time.

Insurgency-related terrorists, which are an insurgent movement conducting an armed campaign against a government using terrorism as a component of that campaign.
State-sponsored terrorism, in which sovereign states, having seen the effectiveness of terrorism as a method of political leverage, covertly sponsor terrorist groups as part of their national policy.

Faced with the challenge of terrorism, national governments initially responded with conventional troops and police, but rapidly found that such groups frequently did not have the methodology, equipment, training and organisation necessary, and there were some expensive and embarrassing debacles. As a result, governments have increasingly resorted to special units, who are trained principally for the counter-terrorist role.

Not surprisingly, different countries have found different solutions. Some have given the role to existing army units (eg, British Special Air Service (SAS)), while others have formed new army units (eg, US Delta), although some have given the role to the police (Finland, Greece) or to the border police (eg, Germany). There are also counter-terrorist groups in other services to carry out specialist tasks, including the US Navy's SEALS (Sea-Air-Land) and the UK's Royal Marine SBS (Special Boat Service). The identity of many of these units, their missions and their actual performance are frequently highly classified by the governments concerned, although they occasionally come to public attention when an operation is, unavoidably, carried out under public scrutiny. Thus, the capabilities of the British SAS in this area were known about only in very general

SELECTED COUNTER-TERRORIST GROUPS[1]

Country	Unit	Service	Remarks
Argentina	Halcon 8	Army	
Austria	Gendarmerieeinsatzkommando	Police	Also known as 'Cobra Unit'
Belgium	Escadron Special d'Intervention (ESI)	Gendarmerie Royale	
Brazil	Projecto Talon	Army Special Forces	
Denmark	Fromandkorset	Royal Danish Navy	Combat swimmers
Egypt	Force 777		
Finland	Osasto Karhu	Helsinki Police	
France	Groupement d'Intervention de la Gendarmerie Nationale (GIGN)	Gendarmerie	
	2me Regiment Etrangere de Parachutiste (2REP)	Army	Used for large-scale incidents only
Germany	Grenzschutzgruppe 9 (GSG-9)	Border Police	
Greece	Dimoria Eidikon Apostolon (DEA)	Athens City Police	
India	Special Counter-terrorist Group	Frontier Force	
Indonesia	Satgas Gegana	National Police	
	Satgas Atbara	Air Force	
	Detachment 81	Army	
	Kesatuan Gurita	Navy	
Ireland (Eire)	Special Branch of Garda Siochana	Police	
Israel	Sayaret Matka	Army	Also known as Unit 269
Italy	Groupe Interventional Speciali	Carabinieri	
	Nucleao Operativo Central di Sicureza (NOCS)	Security Police	Also known as 'Leatherheads'
South Korea	707th Special Mission Battalion	Army	
Malaysia	Unit Timpa'an Khas	Malaysian Police	
Netherlands	Marine Close Combat Unit	Royal Netherlands Marine Corps	
Norway	Beredskastrop	National Police	
Pakistan	Special Servies Group	Army	
Portugal	Grupo de Operacoes Especialais	Public Security Police	
Singapore	Tactical Team	Police	
	Special Operations Force (SOF)	Army 3 platoons	1. Co. strength: 2. Formed in 1984
Spain	Grupo Especial de Opereaciones (GEO)	National Police	
	Grupose Antiterroristas Rurales (GAR)	Guarda Civil	
Sweden	National Rescue Group	Police	
Switzerland	Stern Unit	Berne	2nd unit is at Zurich
Turkey	Ozel Inithar Kommando Bolugu	Army (?)	
United Kingdom	Special Air Service (SAS)	Army	
	Commachio Company, Special Boat Service (SBS)	Royal Marines	
	Unit D11	Metropolitan Police	
USA	Delta	Army	
	Hostage Response Team	FBI	

[1] Sources: The World's Elite Forces, Walter N Lang, Salamander Books 1989, p14; Jane's Defence Weekly (various issues).

terms until they broke the siege at the Iranian Embassy in London on May 5 1980. Because the siege had been going on for some days and the embassy was in a public road in London, the Press was already present in strength and it was unavoidable that they should broadcast them in action.

LEFT: US Marines guard their Beirut base after many of their comrades have been killed by a terrorist bomb.

OUTLOOK FOR CONFLICT IN THE 21st CENTURY

Potential trouble spots during the 21st Century

1. Quebec
2. US/Mexico border
3. Mexico
4. Cuba
5. Colombia
6. Brazil
7. Peru
8. Argentina
9. Falkland Islands
10. Northern Ireland
11. Belgium
12. Basque Country
13. Western Africa
14. Central Africa
15. Southern Africa
16. Madagascar
17. Kaliningrad
18. Former Yugoslavia
19. Albania
20. Greece
21. Libya
22. Turkey
23. Cyprus
24. Israel
25. Kurdistan
26. Iraq
27. Kuwait
28. Saudi Arabia
29. The Gulf
30. Iran
31. Straits of Hormuz
32. Afghanistan
33. India/Pakistan border

The art of forecasting is notoriously imprecise, but this brief study of the campaigns of the past one hundred years may at least give a few indicators for the next century.

First, some existing campaigns will simply drag on because the situations are insoluble, particularly where a minority is seeking some sort of autonomy. Minorities simply cannot be disposed of, either by moving them away (as Stalin tried with the inhabitants of the Crimea) or by eliminating them, which is genocide. Thus, it appears unlikely that the current conflicts in Afghanistan, Cyprus, Northern Ireland, Kurdistan, the Basque region of Spain, Sri Lanka and the former Yugoslavia will continue, as will less well-known revolts, such as those in Burma (by the Karens who have been fighting since 1949), and in Tibet. Similarly, the many minor conflicts in Central Africa appear likely to continue for many years to

34. Kashmir
35. India/China border
36. Tripura
37. Kachin
38. Burma(Myanmar)
39. Straits of Malacca
40. Sri Lanka
41. Spratly Island
42. Pracel Islands
43. Taiwan
44. North Korea
45. Salkhalin
46. Kuril Islands

come and new ones will undoubtedly arise.

One of the lessons of recent history is that states formed from disparate ethnic groups will tend to survive so long as there is a very strong central government. But, as the break-up of the Soviet Union and Yugoslavia have shown, as soon as the power exerted by that central authority weakens, domestic trouble starts and accelerates until centrifugal forces come into effect with groups, especially at the periphery, demanding their independence. Thus, if centralised control in China were to hesitate, substantial independence movements could develop very rapidly.

The past ten years in Europe have shown that it is feasible for older states the hive off elements of the states in a peaceful fashion. Thus the end of the Cold War led to the Soviet Union returning sovereignty to old states such as Estonia, Latvia, Lithuania and Ukraine in relative calm, while Czechoslovakia split into the Czech and Slovak Republics in a most peaceful manner. Other situations are, however, less easily solved and the intransigence of the participants means that either violence or the threat of violence will continue.

Further, with the increasing fashion for the break up of sovereign states, it may well be that many more ethnic groups will seek an independent state of their own, and, if thwarted, they may turn to violence as the only answer. Thus, existing and currently relatively peaceful independence movements may turn violent in Belgium, Quebec, Scotland, Wales, and in other countries where such movements are not at such an advanced stage.

All the countries split for Allied convenience at the end of the Second World War have reunited, except for one, Korea, where a particular

danger exists. The most beneficial outcome would be a sudden implosion in the North, leading to a peaceful takeover by the South, as happened in Germany. However, the increasingly erratic behaviour of the northern leadership as it loses its grip on the country may lead to rash operations resulting in war with South Korea.

Other flashpoints will continue to contain at least the potential for violence. China, for example, will never be deterred from its intention to recover Taiwan, and the return of Hong Kong (1997) and Macau (1999) only reinforce this. China will also pursue its claims over the disputed islands in the South China Sea,

including the Spratly and Paracel groups, and its aim to be the first Asian superpower may bring it into conflict – possibly armed – with other major states in the area, even, in the long term, the USA.

Certain neighbouring states seem destined for virtually perpetual animosity, with an ever-present potential for war. These include: India and Pakistan; the Arab states and Israel; Greece and Turkey; Iran and Iraq.

There are a number of currently unresolved problems. One is at what stage can the UN or some other outside power interfere militarily in a country's domestic affairs? The USA, for example, used military force in Panama, and then arrested and extradited former President Noriega to the USA for a trial on drugs charges. But, if, say, some future US government considered it necessary to eliminate the drug producers in Colombia and was faced by a non-cooperative government in Bogota, would similar force be justified? Also, quite apart from drugs, how long must outsiders allow a country to tear itself apart in a civil war without interfering? If, say, the state of Zaire was to descend into another bloody civil war, would any country or group of countries wish to interfere to stop the killing?

Iraq, North Korea and Libya continue to act as 'loose cannons'. Iraq continues to threaten the peace of the Middle East and there is no point in trying to forecast what Saddam Hussein might do in the future, since he has shown in the past that his actions are totally unpredictable. Libya has been relatively quiet since the US air attack on April 16 1986, but the underground chemical plant at Rabta is now reported to be in production, although

where and how the resultant weapons might be used has yet to be demonstrated.

Much has been made in the last ten years of the great benefits offered by modern technology, especially in its ability to carry out surveillance, and thus warn of military threats. It is, however, worth recalling that high technology surveillance and warning systems did not prevent surprise military attacks taking place, as, for example, when the Egyptians crossed the Suez Canal (October 1973), the Argentines invaded the Falkland (Malvinas) Islands (1982) and Iraq invaded Kuwait (1990). With the benefit of post-conflict analysis (hindsight) many markers were found which either individually or collectively should have told observers what was going on, but they were either missed, deliberately ignored or used to arrive at false conclusions.

If forecasters had been asked in 1980 to foretell what the world might be like over the next 15 years and they had suggested that the USSR would have collapsed and split up, that the Warsaw Pact would be but a distant memory, and that NATO troops would have deployed to Yugoslavia with Russian troops under command, they would have been considered unbalanced. If they had then added that Britain would fight and beat Argentina in the Falklands (Malvinas), and that a grand coalition of Western and Arab contingents would deploy to Saudi Arabia and defeat Saddam Hussein in just 100 hours, they would have been laughed at.

Thus, to attempt to forecast what conflicts might happen in the 21st Century, let alone over the next 15 years, would be singularly ill-advised. Of some things, however, we may be certain: there will continue to be conflicts throughout the world, and governments and people will continue to be taken by surprise by their timing, location and nature.

BELOW LEFT: Africa, too, remains high on the list of the world's trouble spots. This Angolan soldier is armed with a Russian machine-gun, one weapon in a vast pool of Cold War armaments widely available - at the right price.

BELOW: Former President Noriega of Panama under escort by officers of the US Drugs Enforcement Agency (DEA). Will the USA seek to extend its reach to combat international crime, particularly in countries which do not seem to be making the effort to exercise their own controls?

PICTURE CREDITS

Jacket: front, top left, US DoD via TRH; top right, Terry Fincher (Photographers International); bottom, US Army via MEL Collection; back, main pic, US Army via MEL; top and bottom, US National Archives via MEL. Page 1, US Army via MEL; 2-3, Soldier Magazine; 5, top IWM via MEL, 2nd United Nations via MEL, 3rd Popperfoto, bottom via Aviation Photographs International; 6, via MEL; 7, US Navy via MEL; 8, top Popperfoto, bottom US Navy via TRH; 9, Popperfoto; 10, US National Archives via MEL; 11, top US National Archives via TRH, bottom, US Naval Institute via MEL; 12-13, top via MEL, bottom left US Navy via TRH, bottom right via MEL; 14, top IWM via MEL, bottom, US National Archives via MEL; 15, Popperfoto; 16-17, top left Peter Newark's Military Pictures, top right and bottom IWM via MEL; 18-19, top left IWM via MEL, top right and bottom US Navy via TRH; 20-21, top left US Navy via MEL, top right Luftschiffbau Zeppelin via MEL, bottom IWM via MEL; 22-23, top RAF Museum via MEL, bottom left/right Popperfoto; 24, top IWM via MEL, bottom Popperfoto; 25, Bundesarchiv via MEL; 26-26, US Coast Guard, Army, National Archives via MEL; 28, top via MEL, bottom Popperfoto; 29, Popperfoto; 30-31, IWM via MEL; 32-33, top US Navy via MEL, bottom Royal Navy Submarine Museum via MEL; 34-35, top left/right IWM via MEL, bottom US Air Force via MEL; 36, US Navy via MEL; 37, US National Archives via MEL; 38-39, top US Navy, bottom left US Marine Corps, bottom right IWM via MEL; 40-41, top left Popperfoto, right and bottom US National Archives via MEL; 42-43, top left IWM, top right and bottom US Navy via MEL; 44-45, main pic US National Archives via MEL, left via Bruce Robertson, right US Air Force via MEL; 46, top US Air Force, bottom US Army via MEL; 47, IWM via TRH; 48, top IWM via TRH, bottom United Nations via TRH; 49, via MEL; 50, via MEL; 51, top US Air Force, bottom US Marine Corps via MEL; 52 and 53, US Army via MEL; 54, US Dept of Defense, bottom US Navy via MEL; 55, via MEL; 56, Soldier Magazine; 57, US Dept of Defense via MEL; 58, National Army Museum via MEL; 59, Popperfoto; 60-61, Popperfoto; 62-63, top/bottom via MEL, right US Library of Congress; 64-65, via MEL; 66, ECPA; 67, top ECPA, bottom Popperfoto; 68-69, via MEL; 70-71, Popperfoto; 72-73, Popperfoto; 74-75, Popperfoto; 76-77, top/bottom Popperfoto, right US Dept of Defense via MEL; 78-79, left Popperfoto, right Royal Navy via TRH, bottom via MEL; 80-81, top, Novosti via TRH, bottom via MEL; 82-83, via MEL; 84, via MEL; 85, IWM via MEL; 86-87, Popperfoto; 88, top Popperfoto, bottom US Dept of Defense; 89, via MEL; 90, Mary Evans Picture Library; 91, Popperfoto; 92-93, Popperfoto; 94, top SIRPA/ECPA via TRH, bottom, TRH; 95, Popperfoto; 96-97, top left, Popperfoto, right TRH, bottom United Nations via TRH; 98-99, Popperfoto; 100, J-P Husson via TRH; 101, Popperfoto; 102-103, Popperfoto; 105, US Marine Corps; 108-109, top TRH, bottom left, Popperfoto, bottom right, via MEL.